PANIC IN THE WOODS

True Stories

Stephen Young

Table of Contents

Introduction

How can someone just disappear in the Woods?

The following true stories, set within the Woods or the most remote wilderness, encompass a baffling and puzzling combination of;

Unexplained disappearances, deaths, séances, assassinations, mutilations, demons, robberies, ghosts; and of course, the most baffling cases of strange disappearances and inexplicable deaths.

Things are never quite what they seem....

Chapter 1: Assassination, mutilations, robberies, ghosts... and a baffling disappearance.

"A New York advertising man's disappearance from a desolate Wyoming highway has all the ingredients of an intriguing mystery novel - except for the final chapter."

The reason The Observer Newspaper said this, on April 12th 1984, is because the final chapter is unable to be written. The mystery itself has not been solved, and it's a complex web of cryptic clues that, despite the passing of more than 30 years, remain ever elusive.

His Mother once said, "This is a horror and no-one should have to be put through this." His sister said; "It was all my fault that we ever went to that house in Maryland. I'm sorry I ever suggested it.... I don't know what everything means. It's all so weird.... The story is so much more bizarre than I told at the time."

It's a true story that encompasses elements of possible Government conspiracy, unexplained deaths of anyone connected to it, UFO's, Séances, an assassination, mutilations, robberies, ghosts; and of course, the disappearance and death of her brother, Don.

"This all started because of a séance at that house, and everything went crazy from there. I still don't like to think about that night."

Her brother Donald Kemp had been working in New York City at an advertising agency. However, outside of work he was a passionate researcher into Abraham Lincoln. In particular, he was most interested in the circumstances surrounding his assassination. So much so that he belonged to a group that shared their obsession for Lincoln, and indeed he had spent much time on his own private research too, with the intention of writing a book about it.

He had only recently partially recovered from a traffic accident, and it was believed that he had been left with permanent injury as a result of it. Whether it was as a result of his slow recovery from this accident, as some have theorized, that led him to abandon the rat-race of New York City and take off for the wilds of

Wyoming, in search of tranquillity; or whether, as he told his friends, he'd made the decision to go there because he intended to finally write his book on Abraham Lincoln and the events that surrounded his assassination. He'd been researching it for many months, and had amassed an enormous amount of paperwork and notes with which he was to construct the book, and that was why his friends and family believed he had headed there.

He left New York City with his car full of his belongings, and headed West. On his journey, he stopped off at a museum in Cheyenne on November 15th 1982. He reportedly spent a couple of hours there, leaving without realizing he had left behind his briefcase.

The next night, his vehicle was found abandoned with the engine still running, on a remote road in a Wyoming prairie, about 40 miles from the nearest town. Don was no-where to be seen. The doors were open and a trail of clothing was strewn across the road. A set of footprints in the snow appeared to indicated that he had walked away across a field.

After his vehicle was reported to local law enforcement, a search was initiated immediately. A duffel bag was discovered some distance from the car, containing items that were later identified as belonging to him, and rather strangely, three of his socks were found 6 miles away in a barn, lying next to a pile of woods which appeared to have been gathered in order to build a fire. Due to a snow blizzard, the search had to be abandoned after 3 days.

During the search, local law enforcement said they found no other tracks in the snow apart from a single trail of footsteps. They covered the area by helicopter too, but again found nothing that would indicate anyone else had been there, but neither could they find any trace of Don. Though they had found the footprints, they did not find a clear trail to lead them anywhere. The trail appeared to just stop after a distance.

The missing man's family asked the Sheriff if a search could be carried out using tracker dogs, but it's believed that he said it was not possible, perhaps because of the blizzard conditions and heavy snow. The police believed he had to have died out in the harsh conditions. He was not in the barn when they arrived there, and he was not out anywhere on the snow covered prairie. Crucially, although a blizzard did come, it had not been snowing at the time his car was found abandoned; the snow arrived three days later.

Five months later, two separate individuals came forward to say they had seen him in Casper, Wyoming, and Cheyenne. Then, a close friend back in New York City received several missed calls. She was out of the city when the calls were made to her apartment, but a voicemail message was left for her, and when she returned and listened to it, she heard Don's voice; or at least, she was absolutely sure it was his voice.

The police did manage to trace the phone number that these calls had come from. They traced them to a trailer in Wyoming. The young male resident of the trailer was a man by the name of Mark Dennis. Unfortunately, he claimed to have no knowledge   of the calls ever having been made, despite them appearing on his phone bill.

The local Sheriff questioned him several times about these calls. He denied having made them. The Sheriff said he felt satisfied with this. The missing man's mother however, was not satisfied. She questioned the young man too, most insistently, determined to get the truth; but again, he was not able to tell her anything, or rather, perhaps the man was not prepared to. The police said they did not have enough reason to obtain a search warrant for his home. He sought out the service of a lawyer, and later, moved away from the area.

It was to be four long years later that his mother was able to have closure; or was she? Her son's body was found, four years later, not far from the spot in which his car had been found abandoned. His body was in pristine condition. It was suggested that he had died of exposure, not long after his unexplained disappearance.

So, perhaps it was a simple but tragic case of a man's unplanned disappearance, due to, as some   have theorized, a nervous breakdown, which caused him to evacuate his car in the middle of no-where and walk off into the distance to his inevitable death in the cold climate of Wyoming. The thing is, the story isn't so cut and dried. It really isn't a story that can be given an easy ending, because it left an array of unanswered questions.

In what had to be a completely unprecedented circumstance, his body had not attracted any natural predators; no animals or vultures had been drawn to his dead body. There was no way that his body had been covered by snow for 3 years – the snow would have melted; and, it hadn't been snowing the night he disappeared. Also, his footprints didn't lead anywhere. Where they stopped, there was no body. When he'd disappeared, he also wasn't seen anywhere during the search. There had been no sign of him.

His friend, Judy Aiello, now a well-known artist in New York, had been Don's co-worker for ten years prior to his disappearance. She knew his voice well. She said that she received 5 calls from him to her phone   line, while she was away. On February 27th 1983, she received two phone messages on her ansaphone. Two more on April 5th, and another one 5 days later. Don's mother said, "She recognized his voice. She said my son spoke in a strained, urgent voice and gave a number where he could be reached."

The artist's number was unlisted. She could not be called without someone already knowing her number. The question is, how could Don have made the call, when the cops believed he had died soon after he'd disappeared? His backpack was found soon after his abandoned car was found; did someone else call her? Someone pretending to be him? Why would they do that? Was it a prank? Was it the guy from the trailer who said he had never met Don? Or, had someone else stolen his backpack?

His sister wonders, "Did this man come across my brother's body and take his possessions including his phone book? This man looked very, very similar to my brother. I looked in high school pictures; they could have been twins. Did this person kill my brother, and take his personal things? Or, could it have been a case of mistaken identity because they looked so alike? They were practically doppelgangers."

When the artist returned to New York, she heard the messages and called the number he had left on the ansaphone. A man picked up, and when she asked to speak to her friend, he said, "Yes," followed swiftly by, "No," and then he hung up. It was the man who lived in the trailer; the man the missing man's mother believed had to be involved. Online over the years, people have put forward the idea that her son was secretly gay and had been experimenting with his sexuality with this man. His sister however, responded to these allegations by stating that he had been a well-liked and handsome man who had been very popular with the ladies. "Don was most certainly not gay. He was very much a ladies man, and, he was engaged." She described him further; "He was magnetic, and extremely intelligent."

While the Sheriff, Captain Mark Benton, said that his investigation into the man in the trailer was "Inconclusive," he also did not pursue the matter further, believing he had nothing to go on. He said the man "implied someone else made the calls from his trailer without his knowledge," but the Sheriff couldn't confirm or disprove this.

The deceased man's mother felt the investigation lacked thoroughness, particularly with regards to this man, and noted that her son's car was not fingerprinted, nor were casts made of the footprints that led away from the car.

The police appeared to be quite keen to go along with the conclusion that he had died of exposure, because presumably they felt they had little else to go on. They were keen to push the theory that he had suffered some kind of mental breakdown and walked away across the Prairie in a protracted act of suicide. The victim's sister however, as well as his mother, were not of that opinion. His mother believes he was abducted by the male who lived in the trailer, or perhaps a different male/or males, and held prisoner in the trailer, then killed. If that were the case however, why were his socks found in a barn 6 miles from the scene of his abandoned car, along with a pile of fire wood?

The alternatives to the explanation that he abandoned his own vehicle and walked away to certain self-inflicted death, is that he was abducted. The problem with this of course lies in the lack of a second trail of footprints, although some sleuths have suggested that an abductor, holding a gun to the back of Don's head, could have stepped in the same footprints as Don to conceal his own. The abductor would have to have walked with a great deal of confidence and carefulness to have succeeded in doing this, and the barn where his socks were found was 6 miles from the abandoned car. Perhaps it's still possible. Some have said that there were only 3 socks found in the barn, because the 4th sock must have been pushed into Don's mouth to keep him quiet.

There has never been an explanation about the phone calls, which could not have been a mistake on the part of the phone company; the calls were itemized on the trailer occupier's phone bill. Had Don been abducted then, and held at this man's trailer? But how did his body come to be found in pristine condition and so close to the scene of his disappearance, yet 3 years after his disappearance?

Locals in Wyoming at the time expressed the strangeness of the circumstances. They didn't think his body would have been left alone by natural predators, and the harsh weather too would have taken its toll on his body before it was found, even if it had been frozen and hidden under snow. Also, how could a body lie out in the open for so long and not be noticed, if, as the police had believed, he had been there all that time? Even though it was a remote location, the land had to be owned by someone? He disappeared when it wasn't snowing, so he couldn't have been buried by snow. Would they have left their land unchecked for 3 years? If he had killed himself, or been killed, his body would have been there and surely would have been found?

Had he been abducted by someone who had blocked his path on the road? Someone with another vehicle who had flashed him to make him stop, or placed a hazard in the road which forced him to stop? Did someone pretend to be a distressed person in need of his help? If so, why would he have been placed back in the same spot 3 years later after he had been killed? And, his body left unmarked and completely untouched? When Don's footsteps were the only ones found, had he fled from someone or something? Had he run in a desperate attempt to get away from someone or something? He was in the middle of no-where. What are the chances a random robber or kidnapper chose to assault him at that spot? How would they know anyone would be coming along that quiet road? Or, maybe they had followed him. Maybe they were following him for a while and specifically wanting him. Of course, if that had been the case, there is still the mystery of the 1 set of footprints that led away from the car and then stopped, and the socks belonging to him, which were found in the barn several miles away.

His possessions were found hanging out of the car and trailing across the road. Had someone come along, stolen his socks and gone to a barn with them? None of it makes any sense at all. His sister has much more information however; but that information leads in an entirely different direction and one that is incredible to say the least. After her brother's death she says, "An expert professor from the Smithsonian Institute in Washington, Dr. Angel, called and   asked for my brother's remains. We approved it and his body was sent there to him. This doctor said that my brother's body was in perfect condition; untouched, and he concluded that there was no way he had been laying in the open for the last 3 years. It was unheard of; he said it couldn't have happened; not with wolves, bears etc. So much has occurred that wasn't known but it is beyond bizarre. Some happened before his death; some happened after his death."

The doctor was a consultant to the F.B.I. and an expert in anatomy and anthropology. "How did this Doctor at the Institute even hear about my brother? What made him contact us? Why did he want to see my brother's body? This Dr told us that his body was totally untouched, and that he had been dead no longer than 1-2 years. There was something else very very strange. I know it was my brother's body because he verified other injuries he had sustained before in his life. Then he told me that his hyoid bone (the U-shaped bone in the neck which supports the tongue) was missing and there was a small perfectly round hole in his head. He was insistent that nothing he knew of was capable of causing that hole. He said he had never seen anything like it. While he said that his body was in perfect condition; he meant it was mummified. I'm just repeating what was said to me."

"Before my brother left for Wyoming, he had given me a book. It was about the Universe. He turned to a page that said 'The Pleiades,' and he said, "I don't know why, but I feel this may be of some importance. You may need this later."

In the same area that my brother disappeared, before we found Don's remains there, there was a U.F.O. group run by a Dr. Springer. They said they were there because of some cattle mutilations. One member of this group phoned me and they told me that they believed "they" -a U.F.O.? had taken my brother. This story is so much more bizarre then I told at the time. They told us they had been camping out in this area due to cattle mutilations and my brother had been 'taken.' They were camped out the night my brother went missing, they said they were researching some cattle mutilations. They called me a couple years later telling me things. I dismissed them as being off the wall; but after we found my   brother and the Smithsonian Doctor told us his findings, I didn't know what to think. I also wondered, years later, how Dr. Angel heard about Don's case; it hadn't been on the TV yet." (This was before the internet and social media. It was also before Paranormal and 'Alien' shows started appearing as mainstream shows on T.V.)

"At that moment, (when contacted by the UFO groups) I didn't believe things could get any more insane; then, all that time later, when they found my brother's body and the Dr. at the Smithsonian examined the body, in his report and what he told me was that he was completely puzzled over both how the body was so preserved, and how the hole had been made in his skull."

"If my brother had just walked out of his vehicle, had a mental breakdown, then how did that account for this Dr.'s findings? Was he killed because someone thought he knew something; something related to U.F.O.'s? - This was two decades before all the Ghost Hunters and U.F.O. TV shows. How did this have something to do with U.F.O.'s? He went missing in the same area as cattle mutilations. His body was mummified. The hole, according to the Doctor was not caused by any animal nor by any known instrument. He told me he had never seen anything like it."

"I had put the book he'd given me on my book-shelf and had forgot all about it as soon as he'd given it to me. The UFO group who'd been camped out in the area and who later contacted me, said they felt that whatever "they" were out there looking for, "they" came from a place called "The Pleiades."- The same word he told me I might need to know!"

"When the Doctor attempted to replicate the wound, he found it impossible. When my brother first went missing, we had calls from lots of U.F.O. people but I just dismissed them all. Then came the Doctor's mystifying findings. What was his interest in the case? I know it all sounds crazy and yet I am talking about the facts.... Then there is also something else which plays its part in this story. Something happened before all this. It was all my fault that we ever went to that house in Maryland. I'm sorry I ever suggested it.... I don't know what everything means.... It's all so weird. My brother had already done years of research into Lincoln when we visited Surratt House Museum in Maryland. There was a woman at the reception and when we went in, she asked us if my brother was the man writing the book. When he said, "Yes," she said she had been told by someone to give him their name and phone number. I hesitate to talk about this because it unsettles me still, but my brother contacted the person and it turned out to be a young lady. She said she was a psychic and she wanted him to come to a séance. She told him she had been "contacted" in regards to the assassination of the President. He said it would be fun to go to and that he couldn't pass that up."

"So, one night we went to her house. He brought his best friend and there was a group of us altogether, including her husband, and we sat around this lady's dinner table. In the center was a Ouija board. My brother had brought with him a tape recorder and he set up a camera to record anything that happened. We began, and the psychic began to ask questions out loud, and the planchette started to move. She then began speaking in a strange voice, speaking with words that were very antiquated; words that we do not use now. She also said things she couldn't have known; unusual names she could not have any prior knowledge of, but that were relevant to us. Some of her knowledge frightened me because she couldn't have known it. Then she began choking and I could see a red line forming across her neck. The room became freezing and the camera began to flick its lights on and off. In the flashing of the camera I could see the shadow of what looked like a woman in the hallway. It looked like she had a long dress on with a bustle in the skirt. The room became colder than ever and it felt as though evil had entered the room.

The room became loud; I know because my brother had to shout over everyone to be heard. I don't know why but there was chaos in the room and he shouted at everyone to get away from the table. He got us all together and he said the Lord's Prayer out loud. I guess he didn't know what else to do, but gradually everything returned to normal again. After that, I never went to a séance again, but I know my brother did because he stayed in contact with this psychic. I know it's easy to dismiss this and laugh it off but I know this was not just hysteria; I was there when it happened. I know what I saw and I know what I felt and I would never want to have that experience again. A lot more happened after this, but I removed myself from it. That evil, whatever it was, it was palpable."

"My brother had done years of research among the archives on the assassination. He told me he had uncovered something very disturbing, but he didn't tell me exactly what it was; he didn't specify. Did he discover something and did someone know he had found something? Or, did they think he had found something? Perhaps it was all coincidence, but I don't know how else to explain all the robberies and break-in's, and deaths."

In 1983, Don's mother asked one of Don's friends if he would go to Wyoming and drive back her son's car. He took a plane and went to claim the car, then began the drive back to Maryland. The vehicle was broken into when he parked it overnight in a motel as he slept. Many of the missing man's research papers were stolen. While parked at the airport, it was broken into again. When the car was returned to the family in Maryland, it was broken into once more, and further personal items relating to his research was taken. When the remaining items were put into storage, another theft occurred. Now, almost all of his independent research on the assassination had been taken. Some of the remaining papers were given to a historian, who died very soon after in a traffic accident. A few audio tapes remained, which had not been in storage or in the car. The family donated these to a man called Mr. Frank Carrington in Virginia. Soon after taking possession of the audio tapes, his house was burnt down with him in it and he died. Other papers which the family still had, were donated to a Civil War store.

According to his sister, "The owner of the store died in an accident, and the papers were no-where to be found. Once all of his research had been destroyed or taken, all of the break-ins and accidents, stopped."

Even stranger, his friend says that when he arrived back at his own home and parked the car outside, he found two coins on the floor. One was face up and had been made in the year his friend had been born. The other was face down and had been made in the year his friend had vanished. Perhaps that was simply a coincidence; but his friend said, "He had a thing about coins. He would say if you find one face up it's good luck. If you find one face down, it's bad luck. As the years have passed, I've continued to see coins when I travel and almost all of them are from the year he disappeared. How do I explain that? I continue to have experiences where I feel he is trying to tell us all something from the afterlife."

Was his family being fed disinformation about UFO's and cattle mutilations to divert the family's suspicions that Don had been silenced because of the information he had said he'd uncovered about the President's assassination? And yet, the assassination happened so long ago, was it really that sensitive if a revelation came out? If it was proof that the official version of the assassination was not the correct one, then perhaps it was. If it was a   disinformation campaign however, how did that explain the unidentified wound in his skull, and the paranormal happenings?

Had Don staged his own disappearance? Had he fled and been hiding out in the barn? Had he been abducted and held prisoner? Why was the Sheriff so reluctant to bring in search dogs? What had his doppelganger in the trailer to do with his disappearance and death? Had he made the phone calls himself, in an attempt to seek help from someone? Where had his body been for the years it had been missing? How had it become mummified? Why could experts not work out how the hole in his skull had been made? What had he uncovered in his research that appears to have resulted in a number of people's mysterious accidents and deaths? How did this tie in with the book he had given his sister, turned to a page about The Pleiades? Was there any connection to the purported cattle mutilations in the area? None of these puzzling questions have ever been answered and his disappearance and death remain an enduring mystery.

Chapter 2: The Case of Arnold Archambeau

On March 10th 1993, two bodies were found in a ditch, 75 feet from the scene of the car accident, which happened 3 months earlier. People had been searching every day for them, in the place where they were eventually found. An extensive and thorough search had been conducted when their car had been discovered, hours after they had crashed. Their bodies were not there. 3 months later, their bodies turned up, in the same place. Where had they been for 3 months? And, why was one of their bodies more decomposed than the other?

In the early hours of a cold December morning in 1992, a car approached a remote intersection on the outskirts of the Yankton Sioux Indian Reservation in Lake Andes, South Dakota. The road was icy. The driver saw that the road was clear, crossed the intersection without stopping, and moments later the car skidded and crashed into a frozen ditch.

Arnold Archambeau, 20, was driving, and his girlfriend, 19-year-old Ruby Bruguier was with him, as well as her cousin, 17-year-old Tracy Dion. Tracy later admitted that they had been drinking and she tried to explain what had happened, but she really didn't know; just that after the intersection, they had ended upside down in the ditch. Her cousin was in the car with her when she opened her eyes, but her cousin's boyfriend wasn't there. Her cousin was crying, she said, and pounding on the door of the car trying to get out. Her cousin managed to ease the door open enough to climb out, but when Tracy went to climb out after her, she says the door slammed shut and she was trapped inside.

Help arrived sometime later and got her out of the car, but at this point, there was no sign of her cousin or her cousin's boyfriend. As inexplicable as it appeared, Tracy could see that they were gone; they had left her in the car and abandoned her. As daylight came, the police had already searched the area of the crash site looking for the two missing teens, concerned that they may have serious injuries. It was freezing outside and they were concerned also of the strong possibility of them developing hypothermia, which would be compounded by shock.

Despite searching both in the dark and now in daylight, the police could see no sign of the two missing teens. Although everywhere was frozen solid, they wondered if the pair had fallen through the ice in the nearby Lake. They could have wandered off, in shock, and unwittingly stumbled across the Lake and fallen in through breaking ice. Given that the trio of teens had been drinking, the deputy Sheriff Bill Youngstrom thought they might have made a quick get-away in a panic that the driver would get a DUI. Officers tracked to the Lake, but found no signs that the couple had walked there. There were no footprints at all. The police had searched the ditch, of course, and all the surrounding area, for miles in the end, and yet they had found no trace of the couple, nor any signs showing the route they had taken.

By the next day, the pair were considered missing people. They had not made it home and they had not contacted their parents, who said it was not in their nature to run away. Besides which the pair, had a young child between them.

The police had searched the ditch, of course, and all surrounding area, for miles in the end, and yet they had found no trace of the couple, nor any signs showing the route they had taken. Over the next three months, the search continued. Then Spring came, and with it came thawing. A driver passing the scene where the car had crashed 3 months earlier, spotted a disturbing sight by the roadside. It was a dead body, lying in the ditch. It was the missing female, Ruby. When the police arrived, they were greeted by the sight of the deceased young lady, now missing both of her shoes, and her glasses, but wearing the clothes she had disappeared in. Although they did not know it was Ruby instantly, by looking at her tattoo they could verify that it was her. Her body was too badly decomposed to i.d. her from her face.

Having found Ruby, they now wondered if her boyfriend could be found in the same vicinity, just feet from the spot where his car had careered into the ditch. The Sheriff instructed the water to be pumped out of the newly thawed ditch. The following day they found Arnold, only a few feet away from where his girlfriend had been found. His body however was not in the same condition as his girlfriend. It was not badly decomposed like hers. His skin was almost pristine. He appeared not to have been frozen in the ground. It was also not confirmed if the clothes he was discovered in were the same ones he had disappeared in.

At their autopsies, both we ruled as having died from exposure. The Sheriff however had an issue with this. In his opinion while they did die of exposure, he was certain they had not died in the ditch by freezing to death there. They had died elsewhere, he believed; In his opinion, it was simply impossible that they had been there all that time since the crash. The spot had been searched repeatedly over the days they had gone missing. There was no way on earth their bodies had been there in the shallow frozen ditch. He, his colleagues too, had covered that ground multiple times. He even instructed his officers to write affidavits of the search effort there, to validate this.

Even more baffling to the Sheriff however, was that when their bodies were discovered, some tufts of hair on the road were found. They were determined to have been Ruby's. Again, it was impossible that her tufts of hair had been lying by the roadside for more than 12 weeks. The Sheriff was of the opinion that the only way her hair could have been there was if her body had been brought back to that spot. Just as curiously, her boyfriend was found to have a set of keys in his pocket that could not be identified. They did not fit his car, nor his home, nor the home of anyone he knew.

One more final twist was added by the polygraph results of a person who came forward to claim that they had seen the missing boy on New Year's Eve, accompanied by three other people. The test results showed that this witness was not lying; or at least, that the witness believed it had been him, at least.

How did the bodies of these two teenagers remain hidden in a shallow ditch that had been inspected repeatedly over the days after their car crash? If the car itself had not penetrated the frozen ice; how could their softer and lighter and smaller bodies have done so? It just wasn't possible that they had been there.

The young lady's father, Mr. Quentin, believed, like the Sheriff, that foul play had been a huge part of this. He believed that someone had taken them, killed them, and brought them back to the scene of their accident. This was in an effort, he believed, to make it look like they had died shortly after the crash. The problem with whoever or whatever did this however, was that the bodies were in totally different states of decay. A shrewd investigator or a parent seeking the truth would not be that easily fooled.

How could their bodies be in different states of decomposition when, if they had died of exposure shortly after the crash, as was the official cause of death, they would both have had to die within hours of the crash and at the same time as each other? One could not have survived much longer than the other; it didn't make any logical sense. One could have survived the crash and found refuge somewhere from the cold perhaps; but there was nowhere around to hide from the elements there, and there had been no tracks or footprints to follow. If they had somehow made it to a house, without somehow leaving any footprints or tracks, they wouldn't have remained missing for three months; but again, there were no houses close enough to walk to anyway.

If they were taken by someone, the dreadful possibility remains then that one of them died quicker than the other. The female was killed but the male allowed to live for a while? Why would that be? And, what must that boy have gone through at the hands of a captor?

If they weren't lying in the ditch all those weeks in winter, then where had they been? And what had happened to them? Why would one, the male, be kept alive, but the female killed? If the witness who passed the polygraph was correct, then the boy had been allowed 'out' in the company of 3 other males. On the other hand, when people go missing, that knowledge perhaps makes us look for them and see people who look like them and get mistaken; wanting to help and wanting to find the missing person, and perhaps at a distance, sightings can easily be mistaken. And again, if he was out on New Year's Eve, why would he not have returned home to relieve his parents and tell them that he was alive? -   unless he was unable to leave the people who were with him; unless he was in fear for his life in their company.

Is this one of the most mysterious cases ever; or, is it simply a circumstance of the ice and cold? Had the female passenger been submerged, somehow, without being noticed by the experienced searchers, while the boy had walked around and later succumbed to the elements? Again, even if she had been hidden from the investigators, somehow, he could not have survived out there for days, and there had been no footprints at all. Had Ruby, who had pounded the door to make her escape, gone in search of her boyfriend, and fallen into the lake and drowned? No, because she was found at the crash site; and there was no water there. And, the lake had been searched, and no tracks were found heading to the lake. In fact, no tracks had been found at all.

Had snow covered them overnight and the rising level disguised the fact that they were now beneath the ice? That again could not have been possible with an active search going on, or could it? Was it   all explainable by ice and snow shift? Or was there more to this case than has never been answered or resolved?

Former Sheriff Ray Westendorf, now retired, called it the most puzzling cases of his two-decade career. He said, "I do know that they weren't there in January." Was their case anything like the previous case, of the missing Abraham Lincoln researcher, with its weird similarities of mistaken sightings, lack of footprints, and the unexplainable conditions of their bodies?

Chapter 3: "Whatever it was, it hitched a ride back to where I live."

Recently I was contacted by a man called Chris Nash. He had a very strange and rather disturbing set of photographs. They had been taken in Rendlesham forest, and at his home, because whatever had been in the forest had followed him home. The photos appear to display a demon. Or, an alien. Whatever it is, the malevolence is clear to see in its yellow eyes amid the darkness of the forest at night. It appears to have an angular face, deep set bright eyes. It is not fully clear but the eyes are there to see. "Whatever it was, it hitched a ride back to where I live, as I've had a presence at my house ever since. Not a nice presence..."

"In the forest I've experienced voices, shadow people, strange lights, the feeling of being sick like death. Personally I had a night where I was walking up a well-known path back to my car and I heard something whisper my name, then I felt a presence. A few seconds later, it was bearing down on my back. After this I had a feeling of being terrified. I was told by a medium I was playing with fire if I kept going back to the forest and something bad would happen if I continued to go. Not that that put me off."

Now however, he feels he may regret his continued visits to the forest at night. "I've got something here at the house that wants a piece of me…. A friend is saying its possibly a succubus, a demon. I heard a growl the other day in my front room, and this morning in bed I couldn't breathe, and it felt like something was pressing down on my chest. I feel like I've got a battle going on in my mind. Is this the battle we all face? Good vs Evil? I'm sleeping with the lights on and it seems OK…..Strange; maybe the light puts them off? I know they love the dark. Demons look like what's in the photograph. Can you see the horns? It looks like a devil; you tell me?"

It did indeed look like a demon. In fact, I've never seen anything quite like or, or as disturbing. It's a very disturbing photograph. A sense of evil pervades the image and it's impossible to deny that it looks anything other than a demon, or alien, but a gut, instinctive feeling leans toward the demonic. It feels very uncomfortable to look at it, as though it is acknowledging it and welcoming its presence just by doing so; as if it is a taboo and cursed thing to do. Perhaps that is just superstition, but then, I wouldn't want to test that theory.

He showed me another photograph; "When I woke up one morning, there was this mark: - there's 6 fingers." The photograph shows six marks on his skin. They look like red finger marks, left on the skin from pressing hard down on it. There are six finger marks, not five....

Chris has been visiting Rendlesham Forest for several years now, sometimes several times a week. It's a couple of hours drive from where he lives to get there, but something keeps drawing him back, despite the warnings and the dark sinister attachment he now seems to have in his house. He took the photographs to a local medium. She insisted he take the photographs out of her house immediately. She told him she would not have them in her house; so strongly did she feel that it was an entity captured in the photos, of a power she did not want to be confronted with.

Though Chris wants help, he feels torn between whether asking for help would make his current situation worse. He says he is torn between exorcism or spiritual cleansing. He fears goading the entity. He also feels he can manage with the situation, but only time will tell if that is the case. Of the entities he says he has seen in the forest at night, he asks, could they all be malevolent or could any of them be good? Like with people, perhaps both benevolent and malevolent spirits or entities occupy the forest. Nature spirits who mean no ill-will perhaps, spirits of the departed returning maybe, but alongside these there may be mischievous and ill-intending darker forces. It's by the East Gate of the forest that Chris and his friends have experienced most activity. It was there he captured the demonic face in the photograph. He said he could feel a presence before he reached for his camera. That presence has now followed him home, and often now, he feels something is standing behind him. In the forest he says he has seen dark shadow people fleeting out of the corner of his eyes; it was one of the first things he noticed in the forest when strange things began happening. He's seen, and captured on film, orbs, and also white streaks that resemble ectoplasm or phantasms. Though he has not seen anything that resembles Extra Terrestrials; several of those in his group have, and on many occasions.

He and his friends began to go there at night, initially drawn to the place after the famous Rendlesham Forest incident. They wanted to explore it at night. Often they would go there, light a bonfire and camp out. They visited other forests too; but this was the one that seemed teeming with activity that does not come from our world. Of all of his experiences there, it is the demonic entity that has most disturbed him. Perhaps even more alarming, Chris says he wonders if the Demon is tempting him. There have been instances where he has had reason to think badly of other people; circumstances in his life, like in everyone's life, where harmonious relationships sometimes turn bad due to the actions of others, and our thoughts toward them become angry. We may even wish them harm: mentally, and even physically.

It's our natural instinct to seek vengeance as our thoughts turn to revenge against those who may have hurt us. In Chris's case, he did harbour bad thoughts towards someone; only this time, he wonders if his negative thoughts turned into reality. He wonders; did his darkest wishes manifest into action? - Someone died, and he'd been wishing them dead. Then it happened another time. He fears there is a spiritual battle between good and evil going on inside his head. He feels he is being offered some form of supernatural power by the entity, and being tempted to take it. He feels the demon may be doing things for him, to prove how much power he could have if he made a deal with it and allowed him in. He even accepts how good it would be to accept that deal, to have that power…..but he won't do that deal.

One of the people Chris goes to the forest with is a lady called Brenda Butler. She's been going there for many years. Chris says she has captured even more images than him; a multitude of strange images in photographs taken inside the forest. Orbs, strands of misty white, faces, dark shapes, and many other unidentifiable anomalies. Brenda Butler has been going to the Forest for decades. She gave a lecture in 2010, in which she described an incident in November, 1979; a year prior to the famous Rendlesham Forest incident, in which U.S. Air-force security witnessed what they believe, was a U.F.O. landing in the forest.

In 1979, Ms Butler was living on a farm at Aldringham (20 minutes from the Forest). "That night a craft came down in the field. It was 3 a.m. My father also saw it. The next morning there were broken tree-tops, and holes and marks in the fields. At the end of November, local people were saying they'd seen UFO's. People came forward to say they'd seen little monks, little people….. A Rabbit Catcher said he saw some little figures. He immediately phoned the RAF base security – he thought they were little children in fancy dress. The RAF security guards came out and went toward them – the figures vanished. The Rabbit Catcher said he was then arrested and taken to the base and questioned. After that, he was reluctant to report it when he had other sightings."

In January, 1980, the UFO reports continued, she said. When she heard of the Rendlesham Forest Incident experienced by the American security guards, she says there were several independent English witnesses to it too. At 11 a.m. on the day after the sighting, a man told her he was out walking his dog when he came across three men in what he said were 'silver' firemen's outfit - or at least, he assumed they were firemen, although he knew British fireman do not wear silver. He said it was bright lights that had drawn him to them, and as he approached the lights through the woods, he hid behind a tree, and from there he could see the three figures. He said he saw a silver 'missile-type thing' on the forest floor, and the three men were covering it over with some kind of tarpaulin. He had refused to talk after this initial report however, said Ms Butler; he was scared, and he said he'd been warned not to talk. He added that he didn't think it was a UFO.

"We've seen greys here," she says. "We've seen them walking. They've stood beside us. We've seen them working – I don't know what they were doing. I think they were building something. They were   taking things away. I think they go to another dimension. Myself and an American have had missing time here - I don't know what happened, but we lost four hours. We were walking down a trail. We saw a big white light. It split apart into 3 lights, then they re-merged into one light. A helicopter came over the trees, chasing it. We were watching it chasing it toward the sea. When we went to leave the forest, nothing looked the same. There were no trees, no familiar sights. We walked for ages and ages. We couldn't find our way back – the area wasn't the same. It was just like open fields. No trees, no bushes. We didn't know where we were or what was happening. Eventually, we did get back to the car. We drove round to where we believed we had been – and everything was normal; the trees, the bushes, everything. I've been with a friend in the Forest, walking together alongside each other and the next minute I'm right across on the other side of the forest; - in seconds I've gone right across the Forest."

"Other people have told me they've been dragged down into an underground tunnel by E.T.'s – I don't believe that. We've looked everywhere but we   can't find any tunnels. There are portals – we have photos of that. I have photos of E.T.'s coming out of the portals."

Given her 30 years of experiences within the Forest, she has written a book based on her investigations, called 'Sky Crash through Time; a continued investigation into the Rendlesham UFO mystery.'

On Sunday, January 25th, 2015, a dog walker believes he captured a UFO in the sky above Rendlesham Forest. He posted the footage on the internet and the BBC contacted him to interview him. Local man George Taylor was walking in the Forest with his dog when he says, "I spotted three balls of light in the sky. Couldn't believe what I was seeing. I had a weird feeling that I shouldn't be there. I recorded it on my phone and uploaded it to see if anyone else witnessed anything similar yesterday. Very strange! Anyone have any idea what it may be? I know the Forest has a long history of this but I didn't really believe in it as I haven't seen anything odd in all the years I've lived here - until this. I regularly take my dogs for a walk here and I've never seen anything as strange as this."

The footage shows three dancing Orbs in the sky above him, above the clouds but in clear daylight. Strangely, there is a low flying helicopter going over the forest at the same time. People have suggested it's a stunt, or a fake, or it's flares; but flares can't behave that way....

Situated 2 ½ hours North-East of London, in the County of Suffolk, Rendlesham Forest is owned by the Forestry Commission and managed by Park Rangers, who maintain the trails and paths, and help walkers if they stray off paths. The Forest is 15 square kilometres in size, and comprised of heathland, wetland and coniferous trees. The Forest is best known for the incident which occurred in 1980, 28 years prior to this man's unexplained footage, and it embroiled the RAF bases Woodbridge, 7 miles away, and Bentwaters, both of which at the time, were home to the U.S. Air-force. Despite the explanations that it must have been a fireball, the light from the near-by lighthouse, freak nocturnal lights, or even stars in the sky, there are those who were at the Bases back then, and who to this day, still stick to the story of what they say really happened.

It was around 3 a.m. on Boxing Day, December 26th 1980, when a night security patrol on the Base near the East Gate saw bright lights in the near-distance, descending from the sky into the forest. The American security guards thought it was an aircraft that had come down, and hurried to get to the crash scene to provide assistance. Within the hour, the local police had been summoned to the forest to investigate, but they felt that the lights in the distance were coming from the Orford Ness lighthouse on the coastline, about 8 kilometres away. The Air-Force security personnel however had seen the lights too, and they believed a small aircraft had descended into the forest. After entering the Forest and going in the direction in which they had seen the descending lights, two of the team came across an object, and it appeared to be a craft mounted on a large tripod.

There were no windows on the craft, but there were blinding lights of red and blue on its exterior. They attempted to approach the craft, but as they got closer, it moved, and each time they attempted to reach it, it continued to move, in a cat and mouse game. It levitated in the air each time, and moved back away from the men. This continued for at least an hour inside the dark Forest, with the men completely baffled as to what it was, and what was happening. They continued to follow it until it edged out of the forest and entered a farmer's field, where it then sped away at incredible speed.

One of the Security personnel, Sgt Penniston, said; "We were sent out by Jeep because it could be a crashed plane. We worked our way to the lights by a logging road. The lights were still visible. We were 200 metres away and wanted a clearer look so we decided to proceed by foot. As we got closer we began to see it was an object with lights on it. We stopped 50 metres from it. Our apprehension was building. Just as we began to close in on it, it began to move away through the trees and the more we moved toward it, the faster it moved off. By the time we were at the field it disappeared behind a rise. We were heading back to base when we saw it coming back toward us; we started to run, but within seconds it was up and gone."

Base commander, Col. Ted Conrad, said of the incident, "He said what he saw was slightly larger than a Jeep and rectangular in shape. Two rows of horizontal lights at the front obscured much of it's details."

Sgt Adrian Bustinza was part of the security night patrol unit who attended the scene. He said that when he arrived at the scene, it was going in and out of the trees and hovering. The next morning, military personnel returned to the Forest and found a small clearing in the vicinity of where the craft had allegedly been seen. There were three impressions in the ground, in a triangular shape, along with burns and branches broken from the surrounding trees. When the police arrived, they expressed the opinion that the marks were caused by 'animals.'

On December 28th, Deputy Base Commander Col. Charles Halt went to the site in the early hours with several of the security personnel, intent on investigating the scene. During the visit, he said he saw separate lights flashing in the field, just as had been seen the other night, and he said a beam of light seemed to reach to ground level. This time, the Colonel had with him a tape recorder in order to log the investigation in real time. He hadn't been involved in the first sighting, but when it happened again, he was interrupted while attending an officer's dinner at the Base, when Lt Bruce Englund entered the room and hurriedly said, "It's back."

The night security patrol had been out and once again seen the strange lights in the sky over the Forest. The Colonel quickly left the dinner and joined the security patrol to go with them to investigate. When they entered the forest, they initially went to the site of the first alleged landing of the craft. They were attempting to get a Geiger counter reading. They were examining abrasions in the surrounding trees. One of the security personnel on the scene says on tape, "The indentations look like something twisted as it dropped. It's very strange."

Col. Hall says, "Looking overhead; can see an opening in the trees and some freshly broken branches on the ground. We're hearing some very strange sounds coming out of the farmer's animals. They are making a lot of noise. They're very active."

Then, the strange lights begin to be seen again. On tape, one of the personnel says, "There it is - there it is again. Red light.... It's coming this way; It's definitely coming this way. Pieces of it are shooting off!"

Col. Halt says, "Flashlights off! There's something very very strange...." They move to try to get closer to the location of the light. "It's moving from side to side. So bright it almost burns your eyes.... We're crossing the field.... Multiple sightings now; Up to five lights...."

"We've crossed a creek. Strobe flashes..... Some kind of phenomenon. The ones to the North moving away, Fast. From the South he's coming toward us..... A beam coming down to the ground.....This is unreal....."

It's now 3.25 a.m. and a check-in call comes from the base. At base, they say they can see nothing on the radars.

In 2013, at a Citizen Disclosure Hearing in Washington's D.C.'s National Press Club, two of the security personnel who were involved in the sighting on the first night, December 26th, gave testimony about what they say happened that night. They described a craft approximately 9 feet by 6 feet, hovering above the Forest floor. Lights were emitting from the craft. Their communication equipment stopped working. They felt a strong static charge of electricity. They approached it, unable to resist checking the curious object out. As they edged closer to it, they said they could see strange symbols on the craft, that appeared to look like hieroglyphics. A blast of light exploded from the craft, stunning them and knocking them to the floor. It was then that they thought they were going to die.

It was what happened next that Sgt Jim Penniston has described as "probably the worst thing I ever did." He walked up to the craft and touched it. It   felt warm, and was smooth, like a glass surface. They both looked under it, trying to work out how it was hovering above the forest floor. It was black, triangular, and glass-like. He said that when it rose to leave, there was no semblance of a conventional lift-off. "There was no sound, no air movement. To this day I have seen nothing like it..." And he remains convinced, "It was under intelligent control."

When they returned to base they found that their watches must have stopped during the incident, because their watches were now showing a time 45 minutes behind what time it really was. They didn't have any more sightings after that, however, it was not long after this that both of them became very ill. They both believe it was as a result of radiation exposure. For Penniston, an inner ear disorder developed too. Later this was diagnosed by the military doctors as Meniere's Disease, a condition of imbalance within the ear which causes dizziness and nausea. He says that in later years, post-traumatic stress set in, along with great difficulty in sleeping.

Decades later, he underwent hypnosis in which he talked about time travelers and the receipt of binary code. Under hypnosis, he said something inexplicable: "They are time travellers — they are us."

He still couldn't sleep and his PTSD continued unabated. At the time of the incident, something else very strange occurred; something which he didn't talk about for many years. He says that when he touched the strange hieroglyphics on the exterior of the craft, he received a telepathic 'download' into his mind; it was an unintelligible binary code of numbers. "They were flashing through my mind and I had a feeling to write them down....so I did and immediately after, the codes were gone from my mind."

He had kept this to himself for many years, he said. When de-briefed, he'd said nothing about it, fearing that if he did he would be declared mentally unfit for duty. But in bed, he couldn't sleep for all the flashes of numbers in his head: "They were imprinted in my mind like a hot branding iron."

He wrote 16 pages of notes - the vast majority of which were an extensive series of combinations of numbers that to him were meaningless. This Binary code, deciphered by Code expert Joe Luciano, was said to include co-ordinates to the Great Pyramids, Sedona in Arizona, and the co-ordinates to Hy-Brasil. Hy-Brasil was a legendary Island in the Atlantic Ocean off the Coast of Ireland. Jim Penniston did not know any of these references at the time. He did not know that among the vast 16 pages set of numbers, would be the co-ordinates of these places including Hy-Brasil. In Irish folklore, this place takes its name from Breasal, and it means the 'High King of the World.'

The Island in fact appeared on ancient Maps in the 1300's, and was situated off the West Coast of Ireland. By the 1800's, it had disappeared from Maps, due to the impossibility of verifying its existence. However, ancient sightings of the Island did exist. Legends said that the Island was shrouded almost permanently in a vast mist, which dissipated for only one day, once in every seven years and it was then that visibility of the mysterious Island was possible. Two Saints spoke of having visited the Island. Saint Brendan and Saint Barrind both said that they had visited there at separate times, and both returned with very similar tales, of an Island of vast opulence, with tall, gold-domed buildings and wealthy citizens. It was believed to be home to a prosperous and highly advanced civilization. The Saints called it 'the Promised Land."

Another documented experience was that of Captain John Nisbet in 1674. He wrote that his crew were shrouded by fog, which as it lifted, showed their ship to be dangerously close to some rocks. They weighed anchor and some of the crew went onto the island which had appeared in front of them. They rowed to the Island and went ashore. Later, on his return to Ireland, the Captain was bearing gifts of gold, and he explained that they had encountered giant black rabbits and a Wizard who lived in a Castle. Not long after that, another party set out to find the Island, under the command of a Captain called Alexandre Johnson. He too returned to Ireland with the same description of having been ashore on the verdant and flourishing Island. In 1684, Irish historian Roderick O'Flaherty wrote of a man called Murrough O'Ley, who claimed he was kidnapped by three men and taken to the Island and kept prisoner there, while a fisherman who also said he had been on the Island, returned saying that he was now able to perform 'psychic surgery' on sick people to heal them, after being given an enchanted book by one of the island's inhabitants.

In Irish tradition, it is thought to be home to one of the ancient clans of Ireland. Some suggest the mysterious Island is not the home of ancient Celtic Gods however, but rather, is home to an advanced Alien race, while others claim it perhaps exists but in an alternate dimension to ours. The telepathic download Penniston received that night from the hieroglyphics he touched on the mysterious craft, once decoded, were the exact co-ordinates of this legendary Island, as charted on ancient maps from the 1300's, and which it is highly unlikely he had ever heard of. The question is, why was he given the Binary code co-ordinates to this Island?

A similar description to the one given by Ms. Butler, about having found herself transported from the Forest to a strange place that was like an open field, is found in this man's account too, as follows;

Luis Serra was on his own, gathering guavas inside the jungle near his village, situated in Maranhao, Brazil. Suddenly he heard a sound like a siren coming from above him, accompanied by a strong light that stunned him and knocked him to the ground. He was unable to move at all; unable to get up or to scream for someone to come to his aid. The light from above pulled him up from the ground, into a large cylindrical object that was above the light. His body was pulled into the object, and he found himself in a room where there were three humanoid forms. He did not understand the language they were speaking. He recognised none of the sounds of the words. The object he was now in began to move, but before long it came to a halt again and he found himself lifted once more, out of the object and back outside of it. Despite being in a full state of terror and panic, he still could not move a single muscle of his body. Only his eyes could move, and he looked around at his surroundings. There was no sky above him, no trees or jungle anymore; instead there was very long, tall grass and above him there was just darkness. It was perhaps some kind of field, but he heard no birds   or any other sounds. He couldn't see the sky and though it was dark, he could see no stars. He fell asleep within moments, after being made to drink a solution of some kind.

When he woke up, he was back in the jungle. He saw the trees once more, and heard the animal sounds. However, he was later to discover that three days had passed. He could move now, just about, but he was in agony. He screamed for help and was heard by a fisherman close-by. Although the fisherman could hear the man's screams for help, he had to search through the jungle to locate him. When he found him, he saw the young man lying on the floor of the jungle, unable to get up. The pain he was in was evident from the expression on his face. The fisherman immediately tried to help him up, but found the young man's body to be completely rigid; his body was later described to be in a condition as though rigour mortis had set in, even though he was still alive. From his mouth, blood was flowing and it appeared that some of his teeth had gone. The young man was unable to speak to explain what had happened to him.

The fisherman managed to somehow lift him up and carry him back to the village, where everyone was stunned to see him alive. He had been missing for several days and no-one thought he would still be alive after several nights in the jungle. They were just as shocked however by the strange condition of his body, which seemed as though it was rigid. Every limb was locked and unable to be moved. Still the young man was unable to talk and it appeared he was in a catatonic state.

He was rushed to hospital, where doctors were baffled by the condition of his body and could also not understand why it appeared that several teeth had been extracted from his mouth. They were also very perplexed by the lack of any marks or bruising or cuts on his body. Apart from the missing teeth, which had caused the bleeding from his mouth, there was nothing visible on his body to explain why he was now catatonic and in a baffling state of rigour mortis despite being very much alive. When his vitals were taken, there was no dehydration despite him having been without any water for several days. He was given neurological tests, which showed no signs of brain damage, seizures, or injury of any kind.

It happened in 1978. Since then, though traumatic for him, he has never altered or deviated in detail when he recalls the incident, and when journalist and Ufologist Bob Pratt interviewed him decades later, the details he gave were the same as his original account. Pratt also went to the police, the doctors, and even the Mayor, who all corroborated and verified that the incident had taken place as described. The journalist related that although the man could remember the incident, at the time he was unable to recall anything until ten days had passed. It was then that he could speak of his experience. Although he was fully conscious for those ten days, he could not speak. When a doctor conducting tests stuck pins into him, his body did not react and remained rigid. He was wide awake all the time, but could only stare into the distance and was unable to interact with anyone. Many of the hospital doctors became involved, including several of the hospital psychiatrists, but no-one was able to explain what his medical condition was, nor what might have caused it...

Chapter 4: Ghost Abduction

In a very odd case, the headlines said: 'A Malaysian Ferry Worker has called in thirty Bomos to solve the mystery of his missing son, believed to have been abducted by a ghost,' said The Straits Times on January 20th, 1956. 'The boy, Maksalmina Mohamed, 3 years old, went missing while playing near his home in Kampong Ringgit,' (4 hours North of Kuala Lumpur.) 'Bomos' are Medicine Men.

His father had organised a large party of villagers and they had searched everywhere in the area, from the small village, through the Woods to the sea, but no trace of the boy had been found. At the nearest police station, they said that the father had reported the child missing several days ago, after he disappeared while out playing. His mother and grandmother had been nearby at the time. While the police were continuing the search for the boy, the Newspaper reported that all of the thirty Bomos (the medicine men) except for two of them, had said that they believed the boy was still living, but was being kept hidden by the ghost, who had kidnapped him. In particular, some of the Bomos said that the boy was being held by what they called 'The Guardian of the Hill.' Almost all of the Bomos agreed that if the little boy was not returned within the next 3 months, then he would never return.

The father and the villagers were inclined to believe the twenty-eight medicine men, who were telling the father that his boy had been taken by the ghost and that he was still alive but being held captive somewhere by the ghost. They all believed this was the most likely explanation. Surely this was just superstition? - A way to find a bogey-man, to explain an abduction that was surely most likely to have been carried out by a person? There appears to be no follow-up story, and so the fate of the little boy is not known, but the villagers all spoke of other incidents where this had happened....

On a paranormal forum, a person asks, "What happens when a person is abducted by a ghost or a spirit? Does anyone know? - I'd rather not go into details of why I'm asking this, but when someone is abducted by a ghost, what are the possible ways   of rescuing the person? And also, once they are rescued, does this person remember their experience? Where has that person gone? And, how is the person hidden by the ghost? How does the ghost hide this person from other people?'

When others on the forum find it difficult to answer his questions, given that it's not believed to be something that can happen to people, he agrees to explain why is he is asking these questions.

"What happened was I was playing hide and seek with my brothers and sisters and my younger sister hid behind a door - I watched her do it. But, when the game was over and she hadn't been found, and we came for her, she had disappeared. She was not there, and she was no-where else. We looked everywhere for her. She was gone for hours. We said prayers aloud for hours, very loudly and continuously. Then she re-appeared from behind the door. She said she had met a huge man...but over the next few days when we asked her about it, she couldn't remember even saying that.'

Beliefs that Elementals and Ghosts can influence and harm humans do seem to exist quite strongly in Malaysia, the Philippines, and Thailand. S. Ging says; 'Things like this really happen…. it's actually true here in the Philippines. People can also be changed into Ghosts or Elementals - they can be changed into a log, or twigs. I know that in the Visaya islands this has happened. People argue between the scientific and spiritual - but it's creepy that this can happen. Souls getting into a person's body is explained as "psychological" by scientists, and while it may sound like scary stories to keep children out of the woods by their parents, by telling them the Woodland Creatures will get them….. it really can happen.'

People changed into logs? How horrifying, and yet surely that is just something that sounds like it is out of a Brothers Grim story?

However, according to Richard L. Dieterle's Hocak Mythology, (Hocak being the Winnebago Siouan-speaking Native Americans, indigenous to Wisconsin and Minnesota) Elementals can at least certainly lurk within the Woods, hiding in trees, intent on mischief.

'Woods Spirits are so-called because they inhabit unusually large trees, especially standing apart. Wakacuna is the name of these Woods spirits, translated as meaning 'The One who Possesses Waka,' with 'Waka' meaning supernatural power. They can take on the material form of a black animal with glimmering piercing eyes. At night when seen, they appear to have fire in their eyes. A Woods Spirit has so much power that if it is simply to thinks of a person then that person will fall ill. If a Woods Spirit gazes on a person, that person will be destined to then suffer misfortune. The Chief of these Woods Spirits delivers life, and dispenses death and dwells in a subterranean spirit world.'

'When these Spirits of the Woods take on human form, they dress in black. One nearly killed a hunter by simply grasping his hand. The Lakota have a similar form of Woods Spirits who lure people into the gloomy depths of the Woods and lead them here and there until bewildered.'

Can Elementals really cause people to become lost in the Woods, deliberately tricked and led to   confusion until they are hopelessly lost and disoriented? Can they really cause those who they turn their focus on to become sick and ill? Investigator of psychic phenomena in the early 1900's, Hereward Carrington once said of Irish writer Elliot O'Donnell, "He was a man about whom it has been said that the gates of his soul were open on the side of Hell." He said this because O'Donnell went through a number of disturbing encounters with, as he put it, "spirits mostly evil and horrible."

O'Donnell said of these encounters, "From time to time I have witnessed manifestations which I believe to be super-physical, both from their peculiarities, and from the effect their presence produces on me. As a child, put to bed but not being in the least tired, the bedroom door began slowly opening. I watched, knowing that my nurse had latched the door, and saw something so extraordinary that I associated it with the Devil; but far from feeling heat, I felt so cold that my teeth chattered. Its eyes fixed upon me with an expression of glee. I do not remember any other features except for the gaping mouth, and that it appeared to have joint-less legs. It approached   the bed and thrust its misshapen head forward. It was the most hideous thing. It did not seem to be composed of flesh and blood. Two weeks later I was very ill.

I told this account at a lecture once, and when I finished, a member of the audience told me that prior to suffering diphtheria he had a similar experience. An apparition had approached his bed and leaned over him. More cases have been reported to me too, in which various phantoms have been seen prior to an illness. I believe certain spirits are symbolic of certain diseases, if not the actual creators. To these I have given the name Morbas..."

He doesn't explain how he came by that name; perhaps it is based on the word 'Morbidity.' O'Donnell also wrote of another odd experience that he had as an adult. "Several years ago, wanting to re-visit the Scottish Highlands, in Perthshire; an area that had great attractions for me as a boy, I answered an advertisement in a magazine for a "Comfortable room offered" in an elderly lady's house. The location   was heavenly, and since there were no other adverts in that area I responded.'

'On arrival my suitcases were taken upstairs by a boy in the MacDonal tartan, and I was given tea of scones and cream. My bedroom was dainty and clean. It turned out that both our ancestors had fought in battalions in Louis XIV's brigades. A week after I had arrived there, I acted upon the landlady's suggestion to spend the day on the Loch. It was a welcome rest from my writing and it wasn't until evening time, around 7 o'clock, that I set out to return to the house. It was a brilliant moonlit night; there wasn't a cloud in the sky, and the landscape around me was as clear as in the daytime; The far-off river, the long range of mountains silhouetted darkly against the silvery sky, the green thickness of the box trees.'

'I mounted my bicycle and rode speedily along the high road, until eventually coming to a stop after a couple of miles. I didn't stop fatigued, but rather because I was entranced with the scenery. I had stopped on a triangular shaped junction where three roads met. I dismounted and leant against the signpost, remaining like that for probably 10 minutes until I was about to remount my bicycle, when suddenly I became icy cold and a hideous feeling of terror seized me. The terror gripped me so hard that my bicycle slipped from my grip to the ground, crashing. The next instant something, and for the life of me I know not what; its blurred outline and indefined shape landed in front of me with a thud and remained there, bolt upright as a cylindrical pillar. Meanwhile in the distance came the sound of a low rumbling, which grew until into view thundered a wagon loaded with hay and on top of the wagon sat a man with a wide-brim hat, talking heatedly to a young boy who lay across the hay. The horse pulling the wagon caught sight of the "thing" that stood in front of me and stopped still, violently snorting. The man cried out to the horse, then in a hysterical screech, "My God! What's that figure boy?" The boy immediately rose up and then clutched the man's arm tight, screaming; "I don't know! I don't know! But it's me it's come for! Don't let it touch me! Don't let it touch me!"

The moon was so bright that as the boy screamed I could see their faces so well, and their expressions were one of abject terror; even more horrifying than the unknown "thing." The gorse, the trees, the grotesque crags of granite, all were overwhelmed by this stillness; the stillness of shadowland. I could count the buttons on the man's coat, I could see the marks of sweat on the boy's shirt. I could see his black nails. I could see the man's chest as it rose and fell rapidly as he breathed fast with fear, and while these minute details were being driven into my soul, the cause of it all was the shock of this indefinable indistinguishable "thing" that stood as a column; silent and motionless, and behind it was a glow.'

'The horse suddenly broke free from the spell of this esoteric figure and it broke off at a gallop, tearing frantically past the phantasm and went helter-skelter along the road ahead, speeding recklessly. The silent and motionless entity now followed in their wake, with bounds, trying to get at them with its long spidery arms. If it succeeded I can't say, because I was uncontrollably frightened that it would return   to come after me, and I rode as I have never ridden before to get away from there.'

'I told my landlady about what had happened. She looked very serious. "I should have warned you," she said. "It has always been that way on that road. No-one who lives here will venture there after dark, and so it must have been strangers who you saw there. It's method never varies. It comes over the wall, remains still until someone approaches, and then it pursues them with monstrous speed. The person it touches will invariably die within 12 months. I remember when I was a child, a night such as you have described. I was coming home with my father from a party. When we reached that spot, our horse shied and we went racing off at terrific speed. I have never seen such fear in my father; his agitation alarmed me so, and my instinct told me this was not from the horse bolting but from something else. Soon I realized what it was; something overtook us and it thrust its long thin arms toward us and it reached my father, touching his hand and then, with a cry that was more animal than human, it disappeared. We could not speak until we reached home. My father was white as a sheet, and he took me aside and whispered to me, "Don't say a word; don't tell your mother what has happened. Never let her know. It was the death bogle and I shall die before the year is out." And he did die.'

She continued, "I can't describe it any better than you; whether man or beast, I do not know, but whatever it was I got the impression that it had no eyes.'

Another account of the harm done by Elementals or Phantasms of some kind, comes from the Scottish paranormal investigator Tom Robertson, only this time, he believes he knows what the entity really was. It began in 1991, when concerned locals contacted him after becoming worried by the number of animal carcasses being found in the woods surrounding Lochmaben Castle, in Dumfries & Galloway, Scotland. The Castle was built in the 1160's by the Bruce family, who were the Lords of Annandal. In the 1300's, Robert the Bruce took it before it was taken back by the English, then surrendered to the Scots again after the Battle of Bannockburn. At the start of the 1600's, the Union of the Crown saw the ceasing of War between England and Scotland, and the heavily fortified castle was no longer needed as a strategic asset. It fell into disuse over the centuries and now lies as ancient ruins which can be wandered through and explored.

Tom Robertson, the paranormal investigator, says he was asked by some of the local people to go there, after they began to get increasingly concerned by the strange incidents of mutilated animals that were being found in the Woods surrounding the castle. He decided to go there at night to see if he could uncover any explanations, and took his wife along for the ride. She perhaps rather sensibly opted to stay in the car, while he took a walk around the ruins and Woods. It was inside the Woods that he claims he saw something he could not logically explain.

It was a figure; "Its eyes as black as coal, its face grey like granite. It was walking about 15 feet away from me. It was a walking, decomposing corpse. Its skin seemed translucent but there were purple veins protruding through its dead withered tissue. It was tall, but it had round shoulders. It had a hood pulled over its head. It took flight suddenly, springing up into a tree and gliding from tree to tree. Then it disappeared... reappeared. Disappeared again... came back, so fast. Concerned for my wife, I hurried back to the car, got in, and drove away fast!"

What happened next, he strongly believes is somehow connected to the thing he saw in the woods. His wife had a stroke the next night, followed by more shortly afterward. She survived, but Robertson had to become her care-giver. It was after she died, that he felt compelled to return to the Castle and the Woods. This time he camped in the Woods. Nothing happened that night, but just before dawn he left his tent and went for a walk through the Woods. It was still dark out and after a few minutes he said he saw a shadow. "It was the 'Vampire,' he said. "It stopped moving and turned its head toward me. Its eyes glared with evil at me. It was grotesque and this creature looked like it had crawled out of a grave."

That should be where the story ends, but then went on to receive a mysterious letter a few weeks later. "It had a postmark from New Orleans. It was from someone who called themselves Mary Grant. She said she had read the Newspaper article (about his experiences in the grounds of the Castle ruins) and she wanted to know if I could catch the creature alive. She said she represented a secret organisation."

He didn't reply. He couldn't – she'd given no return address. The letters from her continued to come. Then, months later, the telephone rang in his house, and when he answered it, a voice with an American accent said, "This is your little friend. You'll have got the letters from Mary. I hope you can help me. I really need your help...." He said the voice was almost child-like, effeminate..... He thinks they wanted immortality. "They must have believed that by taking the blood from this creature that had lived hundreds of years, they could transfer its regenerative cells, in an attempt at gaining eternal life."

"I never went back to the Castle....and nor should you," he warns. "There is a creature there in the Woods. When it happened, I felt something; a presence. It wasn't spiritual it was physical, but I could hear no footsteps. The hairs on the back of my neck stood up. I turned slowly and it was there - the most hideous thing. It disappeared - then reappeared. Again and again."

Was it this creature that had been mutilating the animals that the concerned locals had first contacted Robertson about?

In the Mountains of Dungiven, in County Derry, Ireland, 59-year-old farmer Gerald says, "They must be getting some twisted kick out of this." He is talking, again, of animal mutilation.

"It is absolutely horrific; there are simply no words to describe it." He is adamant that the attacks are not the result of an on-going feud or an argument with anyone in the area. "We have no quarrels with anyone, there is no reason in the world why someone would do this to us?" He and his wife Bridget say there can be no doubt, that it is a person responsible for the hideous crimes. "Who would even think of doing such a thing to young lambs. You cannot imagine what is inside that person's head."

The lambs are his livestock, and over 500 sheep on his farm have been attacked. All have had to be put down. This is no new thing however; astonishingly, it's been happening for the last 20 years. That would be a long time for a person to hold a grudge, and to carry out this kind of activity. The husband and wife have a flock of 300 sheep; but they are constantly having to put them down – because they are consistently being attacked. They have reported it to the Police, to the RSPCA (Royal Society for the Protection of Animals) and countryside Agencies, all of whom have carried out extensive investigations and yet found nothing to explain what is happening to the animals. A police spokesman said, "Police have received numerous reports since 2000, of sheep mutilations at the farm." However, they added that they have found "No evidence of any offences having been committed, and no suspects." In fact, the police are baffled, as is every agency that tries to investigate.

While the farmer believes it is some kind of sick individual who is doing this, a near-by cow breeder came forward with the theory that the culprits could be hooded or grey crows. This the sheep farmer instantly dismisses; "Since this all began, we've kept records and photos. If it were crows, why would it just be my fields? If it were wildlife, why are other farmers not losing sheep like we are?"

Now, almost twenty years after it began, he wakes every morning in dread of what he will find when he goes out to his fields. With predictable regularity, he will come across the horrific sight of young lambs who have had their tongues mysteriously cut out.

"These lambs are still alive after their tongues are cut out. We have to put them down - they would either bleed to death, or they simply wouldn't be able to eat to survive." In total, he has now lost more than 400 sheep; all of them attacked in the dead of night in what the farmer calls "An evil, barbaric act." Even though they have stayed up some nights, trying to catch "whoever" is doing this; they have never seen anyone in their field; yet still, when they go out to the fields in the morning, they will find mutilated sheep. "I even employed security to look after the place overnight. They found nothing and it cost me a fortune. We have tried many times to catch whoever or whatever is doing this but have never found anything."

At Easter last year, fifteen sheep were attacked over the course of three weeks. It even seems to happen in the daytime. "Our house is a short distance up the road from the farm buildings. When we went home for some coffee, someone or something entered the shed and two young lambs had their tongues cut out. It has never stopped."

Wales too saw mysterious animal mutilations in June 2016. The Daily Post wrote of a 'surgical wound' found on a young lamb in Beddgelert, which the Newspaper says 'sparked formation of alien investigation unit.' The lamb was found dead on a farm, with an oval-shaped hole in its hip bone, which appeared to have been so cleanly cut that it led to the belief that it had to have been cut with some kind of surgical instrument. There was 'trepanning of the bone;' that is, it was as though it had been drilled. 14 years prior to this, at a farm in Plwmp, in Dyfed, Wales, six ewes had been found in the most horrible condition. Their jaws had been stripped of flesh and their tongues cut or torn out, yet there was no blood on the scene. In Monaught, Wales, four ewes were found dead with the same wounds.

Phil Hoyle, who was part of a paranormal and scientific group which had formed to investigate the incidents, cited the strange lack of any blood, or tracks, or footprints at the scenes of the mutilations, despite the removal of significant tissue and flesh from the animals. He went on to point out that they were not ruling out the possibility that it was something other than a wild animal or people, who had done this.

"We are looking into things people have described – some farmers have seen unusual and unexplained lights, some people have described seeing unconventional things; things that they say they have seen entering and leaving the sea. Farmers are finding animals killed in a very surgical manner. This is not being done by satanic cults. This is very sophisticated. Whether it's done by aliens, military, or some kind of clandestine monitoring; something is going on that is very unusual. Very often they are drained of blood."

The most rational explanation offered is that natural predators, including insects, can produce injuries which appear to look surgical. Some experts say that when an animal has died, its body will naturally bloat and that this swelling can cause its skin to split, making it appear that there is an incision, and that after the skin has split, it will give natural predators access to their internal organs, and that as such, when internal organs are missing, it may well be that they have been removed by these predators who are scavenging, rather than the more dramatic explanation that it is from alien intervention. However, while that is a perfectly good scientific and medical explanation, it still doesn't answer how such wounds appear to be so cleanly split, and the cuts so incredibly precise. Surely a highly experienced veterinarian would be able to tell the difference, and yet in almost all of these cases, that is not so. The verdict is usually that they have never seen anything like it, and cannot say how it could possibly have been done.

John Duggan, who owns a large sheep farm near Knighton, an area where more mutilations have occurred, has the opinion that there is nothing sinister and believes there is a perfectly reasonable explanation; "We find sheep dead or carved up, but when we find them usually they have been killed by wildlife, like birds. Nothing surgical – it's just you might not be able to find it for two or three days." In other words, his version would tend to suggest the natural splitting of the carcass after death, although why he said 'carved up,' is strange.

Hoyle, who's been looking into the cases for over 30 years in the area, which he calls a mutilation 'hotspot' however, says, "What has the ability to do this? - to literally walk into an isolated rural area, surgically remove tissue, then walk out – without leaving a footprint." He claimed that the Military were in the area, monitoring things, although the Ministry of

Defence say this is not the case, commenting that "There is no benefit in such investigation."

In May, 2012, the headlines of The Telegraph said; 'The Beast of Bont returns near the Devil's Bridge in the Cambrian Mountains near Aberystwyth, Wales,' after 20 sheep were found 'massacred.'

Their mutilated carcasses were torn to shreds and scattered across the moorland near Devil's Bridge. This was not the first time it had happened, and many locals believe there is a Beast who roams the area; a big cat perhaps, and reports of sightings of an unknown predator have been recorded there for the last four decades at least.

However, one local man and his partner were out for a walk when they came across a macabre sight. Mark Davey, 43, and Annette, 41, came across the dead animals with no warning, and both insist that this was not the work of a fox or a dog. Describing it as "sickening," Davey explained what they saw.

"The whole area stank of dead animals. There were body parts lying everywhere. They had been   ripped apart. At first we thought maybe it could have been a fox, or badgers, but the increasing number we came across started the alarm bells ringing. It was as though some sort of large animal had attacked them. There were several all lying close together. We were walking in remote land high up in the mountain. At first we saw a couple of dead sheep. We walked on and entered some woods and then we saw more dead. As we walked through them all, we began to get scared ourselves; we couldn't think what the hell could have done this. They had been stripped bare - there was just piles of wool, and bones. Some were lambs. Something had clearly ripped them apart. Some of them had just half bodies, or just legs left in the field. I also saw a lamb which looked to me as though it had been carefully placed in the corner of some ruins." Chillingly he says, "It was untouched. To me it looked like it had been put there for a reason - maybe to come back to later."

In the '90's when this was also happening, Vets from the Ministry of Agriculture came to the area to investigate the numerous incidents of sheep that were being killed, swiftly and with the utmost savagery. After examination, the Vets declared that whatever killed them was a great deal more powerful than any dogs or foxes, but they also had no idea what it was.

Chapter 5: True Detective or the movie Deliverance?

"Southern Detectives "want Cult victims to Return," said the Headlines in the P.A. Morning Call Newspaper, in 1994.

It said that the authorities had not yet decided their course of action with regards to two young men from East Penn Township, after they had apparently been chased across rural Tennessee and Arkansas and one of them abducted by a 'strange cult.'

It came just a year after the horrific 'West Memphis Three' mutilation and murder of three small boys in rural Arkansas, after which Damien Echols was sentenced to death for his part. Much later, Echols was freed from prison, along with the two other young men who'd been found guilty of the boys' vile murders, which many believed was driven by dark occult and satanic beliefs.

Now, 12 months after these boys' deaths, Heath Bullard, 23, and David Smith, 25, were to describe an experience which sounded like a cross between   the hit TV series True Detective and the movie Deliverance. The nightmare for Heath and David seemed to begin when they were pursued by a convoy of vehicles on August 9th 1984, while en-route to Arizona. Heath was taking his best friend David with him for a short break before Heath began a student teaching post. He was an education major at Kutztown University in Pennsylvania, and David was a painter with a trade union there. They were headed to Texas first, where they were going to spend a few days on vacation, and then drive to Arizona, where David would fly home, while Heath would stay to begin his student teaching.

Best friends since childhood, they were looking forward to their road trip, but that road trip quickly descended into a nightmare that according to them, they barely got out of alive.

They later explained that it began when they were simply driving along the highway and a convoy of vehicles began to tail them. The convoy, according to them, was comprised of multiple vehicles, including tractor-trailers. They were in Arkansas at this point.

They said they fled through the State, crisscrossing roads and back-tracking, trying to shake off their pursuers but to no avail, and they ended up in the Lauderdale and Tipton Counties of Tennessee. Prior to this, the two men claimed they had tried to get help, at one point stopping in the small hamlet of Prescott, Arkansas, where they approached the Sheriff. The Sheriff's response to them, they claimed, included accusations that they were high on drugs, and he asked them to show where their pursuers were. The two young men pointed out one of the vehicles, to which the sheriff said, "They're locals;" implying they were doing no harm. He told the boys to go away with their tails of being followed by 'ghost' vehicles.

The Morning Call Newspaper contacted the Sheriff, who said he had had no contact with the two boys. The two boys left town, and drove on, convinced a convoy of vehicles were still chasing them. They didn't stop driving for more than 250 miles. When they approached the Texas border, they claim three vehicles of tractor-trailers boxed them in and forced them onto an exit ramp, trapping them. They had no choice, the two young men said, but to drive back into Arkansas. Once they had gone a fair distance, they stopped their truck on the side of the highway and a State Trooper found them. They explained what had been happening to them, but said that the trooper just laughed at them and said he couldn't help.

They drove off once more, this time going across the border into Tennessee. By now, it was getting dark and they were close to running out of gas. As they drove on they struggled to find an open service station. That's when two cars, "that looked like cop cars" they said, "chased us into a field."

Forced off the road and into a field, the field was very muddy and their truck got stuck. Terrified, they fled the vehicle. It wasn't just one car chasing them; they said it was close to 30 cars, trucks, and tractor-trailers, all in pursuit of them, having chased them from State to State, for hours. As if that wasn't bizarre enough, things got much weirder; David and Heath said they jumped from their truck, leaving all their belongings behind and ran for their lives. Fleeing on foot, running as fast as they could, they ran without any clue where they were heading but were too terrified to care. The hoard of vehicles they said were behind them were full of people, and they clearly didn't have intentions that were good.

The two young men ran into the night, into some woodland; separating when they reached a creek. Heath described their panicked escape.

"My legs were scratched and cut and bleeding. I started to puke. I didn't have any water. We reached a creek. David swam. I couldn't swim so I hid. The next minute I was being chased through the swamp. I had to take off my boots – they were too noisy. I was hiding. I stayed in the swamp that whole night and most of the next day." His pursuers were moving through the swamp, hunting for him and communicating with him by bird calls, he said. Finally garnering the courage to leave his hiding place in the swamp, he says he walked mile after mile until he came to a farm.

"When the sun rose the next morning I couldn't walk anymore. My stomach was in cramps. I had to have a drink." He kept away from the entrance of the farmhouse for a long while, afraid of who was inside and feeling unable to trust anyone after his experience of being chased all night through the swamp by his unknown pursuers. Sometime later, he said that a woman came out from the farmhouse and offered him a drink and asked if he was ok, and asked if he would like to come inside and take a shower. She gave him clean clothes and he then used her telephone to call his family and ask them to wire some emergency funds to him so that he could fly him. The kind lady even went into town for him and collected the money that had been transferred, as well as arranging for his safe transport to Memphis airport, where he got on a flight as quickly as he could. He just wanted to get out of town as fast as he could. He never wanted to go back to the hell he said he had experienced that night.

Without knowing where his best friend was, or if he was ok, he fled the swamplands and headed back to the safety of his family. Once there, he described his experience, expressing confusion and disbelief that no-one would help them when they were being stalked by the convoy of vehicles.

Once home, he stuck to his story. He repeated that they had been followed for mile after mile by a huge convoy of vehicles, chased from State to State, and eventually forced off the road into the mud-filled field. In fear for their lives they had fled on foot, until eventually splitting up when he became ill and his best friend saw no other option than to jump into the river and swim for his life. He hid out in the swamp in the pitch dark, craning his ears for every sound of the footsteps searching for him, dreading the moment they found him, until light eventually came.

As for his best friend David, who he got separated from when David jumped into the river, things had got much, much worse. Later, as his mental condition deteriorated, he stuck to the same story he first told when it happened. He described what had happened to him. He said that he was chased through the swamp by his pursuers, who shot pellets at him. It wasn't just men; he said there were women chasing him, and children too. Entire families it seemed. He swam and grabbed hold of a log with which he floated downstream, and was asked by a man in a boat at some point if he wanted help, when the man saw him clinging to the log in the middle of the river late in the night. David declined the man's offer of help however; he didn't know if this man might be part of the group chasing him too, so he refused and carried on drifting down the river.

He must have got out of the river at some point later that night, but that was where things became even weirder. He said that he found himself surrounded by the people who were hunting him after they managed to track him down in the swamp. They surrounded him and abducted him. He was not able to leave. He says they were joined by more people, who stood and watched as the members of the group closest to him slaughtered pigs and sheep and rolled around in the blood. He was forced to watch. He said he saw decomposing human heads hanging from a tree. He said that the members of this group were wearing two white patches on their shirts. On one of the white patches was the letter 'A,' and on the other white patch was an image which appeared to be in the form of a Witch. They led him away out of the swamps, and took him to a tiny Church in the middle of nowhere, where he says he saw the same images of the letter 'A' and of Witches, hanging on poles.

Somehow amid the orgy of blood-letting, he managed to break out and run for his life. After a mile or so he came upon a house. He broke into the house, grabbed some mail to find the address of the house and quickly phoned his girlfriend to get her to call the police. She contacted the Sheriff's office in Tipton county, and the deputy Sheriff duly arrived at the house with more police. Unfortunately for David, it seems that the house he had broken into was owned by a policeman. The officers took him to hospital after seeing the state he was in, where he was treated for dehydration. Not long after he arrived there however, he ran out of the hospital and got a ride to the airport in Memphis. The Sheriff's office said he was discharged from the hospital; while the hospital said he had never even been there.

At the time this was all going on, Captain Charles Yoakum of the Sheriff's department, as well as the

County Sheriff of Lauderdale, Tim Sutton, apparently confirmed some small facts about the case, but laughed-off the vast majority of it as madness.

The Tipton Sheriff said at the time, "It doesn't make a whole lot of sense; a 30-vehicle car chase, for so many miles? It's unreasonable to believe it...I have no earthly idea about this." He also said, David had not phoned for help; that rather, it was neighbors who phoned police, concerned that there was a prowler in the area.

"Residents out there kept calling in, saying someone was around. They said there was someone around, something on the loose, something strange. Our Lieutenant found him while doing a search."

In a strange twist of fate, David had indeed broken into a policeman's house. At the time, the Sheriff said he would not face prosecution for it. However, this would later change. The Sheriff said at the time, "The more serious violation is the wild tale he told us."

When asked by the Newspapers if he knew of this strange cult in his constituency, his response was,

"It's just not plausible. Possible? – Well, anything is possible; but it's not reasonable and certainly it's not plausible at all. These two boys said they were chased from one State to another, hundreds of miles, from Tennessee to Arkansas and back; by a convoy of up to thirty vehicles!"

He agreed that there was indeed a small rural Church in the vicinity of where David said he had been when he'd fled to the policeman's house, about a mile from the Church, but he said it was a regular church. "It's just a small old county church; in an extremely rural area. I don't know the denomination of it."

His opinion of the wild and outlandish tale, he said, was that they may have believed the flow of traffic behind them was following them, but anyone lucid would not turn that around and say they were being followed! By that many vehicles! I suspect there's more to this whole thing than we know at this point."

Sheriff Sutton, who's jurisdiction falls within the area where the two boy's had their ordeal, confirmed at the time of the incident that their truck was indeed found in a muddy field off the highway, and it had been driven way into the field, so it did not appear an accident but rather a deliberate move on the part of the two boys. Inside were all of their belongings including a computer and other valuables.

The Sherriff made the comment at the time; "Tell him it's ten bucks a day for storage, and he can't get it until he talks to us." He also said he had found no other tire marks that would indicate any other vehicles had been in the field. Nor any tracks from people. "It was so muddy no other vehicles could have got down there."

This Sheriff said, "We got a report of two boys being chased from another county, we got a report of a man floating down the river, on a log, then a guy came in and said he was in a boat and offered to help him but he said he didn't want any help."

When he too was asked what he made of the strange case and the allegation of cult activity in his county, his response was just like the other Sheriff. "Pig and Sheep blood? Human heads hung on trees? Ain't nothing like that round here. That sounds kinda crazy. We've had a little touch of cults, just reports, you know, and gang stuff, spray painting and stuff but that's just crazy."

Were these two young men crazy? What on earth could have driven them to make up such a ridiculous story? Going so far as to abandon all of their belongings and valuables in the truck and run off? Was there any way their story could have had any elements of truth in it? If they had been chased into the field, after hundreds of miles of being terrorized by a large convoy of vehicles, why were there no other tire marks or vehicles in the field? Why were there no other vehicles also stuck in the mud? Or, had the other vehicles known that venturing into a mud-drenched field would result in their vehicles becoming stuck, particularly if they were local to the area? Had they entered the field on foot instead, to pursue their prey?

Had the two boys made up the story because their own truck had got stuck in the mud and they wanted a free tow? But then, why would they even have driven off the highway, down side-roads and into a field? If they had, why would they have separated that night and one of them swum downstream in the river clinging desperately to a log while the other hid in the swamp all night? A fisherman in a boat had confirmed independently, before the two boys had been found, that he had come across a boy holding onto a log and floating down the river.

Were the two boys high on drugs? Had they been drinking alcohol? After David had been found at the policeman's house, he was tested in the hospital for alcohol and drugs; none were found in his system. He had been completely sober at the time of their desperate night-time escape.

David said they had been pursued into the swamp, that he had been captured by a crazy cult made up of men, women and children. In David's opinion, the reason for the police laughing off his claims, is a rather sinister one. He believes it's because the Sheriff and the police were involved in the cult themselves. He told reporters he had not got his story wrong. That despite not sleeping, eating or drinking for two days, his physical condition did not affect   his understanding of what had been going on. He also said he was not paranoid and had not "imagined it."

He added that his story in regards to being chased by a crazy cult did not differ to his best friend's account, despite the fact that they had been separated for much of the encounter with the cult, and had not conferred.

"If two people become paranoid, or delirious, or sleep deprived, you'll get two different stories. What we saw is what we saw. We did not misinterpret what went down."

On his return home, his parents and girlfriend met him at the airport, alarmed at the cuts and scratches all over his body from the time he had spent in the swamp. His girlfriend then told reporters that she had received a desperate phone call from him, telling her that he had been held hostage in a house in Tennessee but had managed to escape. She confirmed that she had then called the police on his behalf. The police however said they had no record of this and that he had not been taken to hospital. They said he had been detained at the police station "for his own protection," implying that there was something going on with his mental state.

When David revealed that a woman whose shed he had been hiding in for a while, shot at him, apparently Sheriff Yoakum responded with; "Sounds like a good move to me."

Fast forward to one year later, and things got even worse. David had stayed in contact with his local Newspaper The Morning Call, and their reporter Tyra Braden. "Weekly therapy sessions have driven thoughts of suicide from his head," she reported, but now, he was facing extradition for burglarizing the policeman's home and assaulting him, and was locked up in the county jail.

It seems that when he managed to find the safety of a house after being chased and abducted by the cult and managing to escape from them, he first went into the shed on the property and found a pair of trousers inside. He changed into them, then made his way to the house. He entered after receiving no answer to his knocks, and used the phone to call his girlfriend to get her to phone the police.

She called the County Sheriff. While David was inside the house waiting for them to arrive, he helped himself to some food and drink, then took a knife from the knife rack and went out to the garage to wait for them.

When he heard a car approach, there was no siren or flashing lights. He did not have his glasses on or his contact lenses in. He couldn't see clearly without them and he later explained that he had picked up the knife in case he needed to defend himself, having not only spent the last 24 hours being pursued by a deranged and blood-thirsty Tennessee cult, but also now being handicapped significantly by not being able to see. His level of terror probably couldn't have got any higher.

When the man got out of the car, he could see no uniform and the man did not identify himself as an officer of the law, David said, and so he raised the knife and began to walk toward the man and the car. He said he could tell the man had something in his hand that looked like it could have been a gun. He dropped the knife to the ground and got to his knees.

The man in front of him was in fact a Lieutenant from the Sheriff's office. David was taken off to jail then taken to hospital to be treated for dehydration. He escaped from the hospital, checking himself out and getting to the airport fast to get out of the county. He said he was told while at the jail that he would face no charges. A year later however, it appeared things had changed. David however, stuck to his story. He said he believed he was being hunted by a crazed cult and that they were going to kill him. He couldn't believe he was being charged when in his opinion, he was just trying to save his own life, having gone through an experience so harrowing that on his return home, he was committed to a mental hospital because of his resulting breakdown; his girlfriend and family became so concerned for his state of mind that they had him admitted to psychiatric care. Was he delusional? - He had never had any mental problems before he went to Tennessee. His family and girlfriend don't think he even told them about the true extent of what happened to him in Tennessee.

David admits he was reluctant to talk about what he went through. He told the reporter, "I just wanted to forget it. I didn't say anything. But things got bad. I read the bible every day now; I never did. It helps me a lot."

What the hell happened to him in Tennessee? -He vowed to kill himself if he was forced to go back there. When he went to leave the psychiatric facility however, he found himself arrested outside and told he was going to be extradited. He said he had done nothing wrong when he was there; That it was him who was the victim, not the policeman who was saying he assaulted him at the house. David says he has the phone records which prove that although he broke into the house, he did call his girlfriend back home, who did then phone the local sheriff's office.

His mom expressed concern for his mental health too. "He said he would kill himself if he was made to go back. He's on medication now to calm him. He just has this blank stare. He says he can't go back there. There's also no reason for him to make up a tale like this. He has nothing to gain from something like this. He'd only be hurting himself and his family. He's scared. He saw something. Something went very wrong. He won't tell me the whole of it. He was never afraid of anything before this happened. He told me he was having nightmares. He said, "Just let it go; I can handle it." There's something he's so afraid of, and I don't know what it is."

Apparently, David was the last to know he was being arrested and extradited. Unbeknown to him, a grand jury had already been convened and indicted him on aggravated assault and aggravated burglary. He admits that he did sever the telephone line after making the emergency call to his girlfriend to summon help, but says that he did it because he was afraid that the people who had been hunting him all night and had captured him, would somehow be able to trace where had escaped to. After all, he was also of the belief that members of law enforcement had been involved in chasing him.

What he couldn't understand was why he was now being investigated and charged, when no-one else was! He couldn't understand why his claims were never looked into properly, but instead were laughed off by law enforcement.

In the end, after having to go through the terrifying ordeal of being sent back to the county in which his nightmare experience had taken place, he was acquitted of the assault charge and found guilty only of trespass, for which he was deemed to have already served his jail time for. He paid a small fine and was able to return home without going back to jail. In order to make it through the trial however, he had to have intensive sessions with a psychologist to ensure he did not completely break down while in the court room.

He said he didn't know how he got through the trial, but somehow he did. Why were his assault charges dropped? Why was his story not taken seriously? Was he completely insane, and his best friend, the student teacher, also completely insane too? How had both of them come up with such terrifying stories of that night which strongly compared, despite being separated during it? Why did they never change their story, or drop it, or admit to having made it up? What would make them think that the local law enforcement had anything to do with this nefarious and sinister supposed cult that hunted people down in the swamplands of Tennessee?

Wild as their story was, they never changed it, and it would seem that at least for David, the mental scars from that night would not leave him. Was it the most preposterous story; to suggest that a highly sinister and blood-thirsty cult had chased them for miles, then hunted them through the swamp? And that some members of law enforcement were in collusion with it? Or, was their experience the stuff of nightmares brought to life?

In Jennings, Louisiana, there are some disturbing and long-standing rumors of some kind of collusion, if indeed not participation in a series of killings that have yet to be solved. The killer or killers are still out there, and have roamed free for more than a decade. The town lies on the edge of Cajun country and paved roads give way to dirt tracks that lead to fields of rice farmlands and swamps. Jennings is a small town within Jefferson Davis Parish near Lake Charles, with a population of about 10,000. Between 2005, until 2009, a series of women's bodies were found dumped in rivers or off the small back roads of the county. Loretta Lewis was found floating in the water in a swamp; others were found in ditches. All of the women very similar things in common. One was that they all hung out at a tiny bar in a rough part of town, and another was that they all had substance abuse problems. Rumors inevitably circulated about their murders through the small populace, and the theory most popular still is that of a local level political cover up with the implication of local law enforcement involvement.

Local law enforcement themselves say that the victims were of different races, and the means by which they met their deaths were varying. What this doesn't do however is detract from the two reasons in which the victims are all connected; by geography and by their lifestyles, the victims are intimately connected to one another. Their drug habit meant that many of the victims were also involved in prostitution.

Some of the victims were found in undergrowth, others half-submerged in canals. Within the small community, as one body after another was found, the fear steadily rose. One of the victims even said she believed she would be the next one to die. When Necole Guillory's mother told her she was planning on baking a birthday cake for her, Necole advised her not to bother, as she believed her fate was already sealed and that she would die within the coming days. She had also put her young children into the hands of family members, asking them to look after the children for her, because she would not be alive to do so herself. Even though she believed she was living her last few days on earth however, she refused to say anything about who it would be that would kill her. She told her mother that in order to protect her and keep her safe, and to protect the safety of her children, she would never reveal who it was that was going to kill her. Tragically, her prophesy was to be proven right. Very soon after that, she was found dead. She was believed to have last been seen entering a vehicle.

Another victim, Laconia Brown, perhaps inadvertently revealed the most telling information when she told her family that she was assisting a local law enforcement officer in his effort to solve the series of murders. She said he was going to pay her for her help and for giving him information. It was not long after she revealed this, that she too was found dead. Brown's sister, Gail said, "She knew what was going on...I think it was a cop that killed my sister." This is according to Investigative Journalist Ethan Brown, who spent two years going through every piece of evidence, speaking to those affected, and reading copious official files. The British Newspaper, The Observer, pondered, was this case "the real inspiration behind the first series of True Detective?"

The victims' stories and the subsequent investigations into their deaths in Jennings indeed again do read like HBO's True Detective, but with very real consequences. Was it a serial killer lurking disguised as a 'friend' or acquaintance' among the dark underbelly of the town, murdering vulnerable and easily accessible young women for the thrill of it? Or was it that the women knew too much about a local corrupt police department, and their killer was actually someone within that office; someone in a position of trust that was meant to protect them?

Private investigator Kirk Menard was hired to look into the deaths on behalf of the families, while law enforcement officers in the area were required to give their DNA. They were asked to do so to quiet the rumors. And all of the victims also knew the owner of the local strip-club, a man called Frank Richard, a former drug addict, who again came under the eye of suspicion. He spoke out on many occasions about the death of his 'friends' the women. "Drugs, prostitution, bars, crooked cops...." he said cryptically. He was very familiar with the marginal criminal underbelly of the small rural town. In fact, it has the highest number of unsolved homicides across the U.S. There are more than just these unsolved women's homicides; there are at least 20 other unsolved murders that also linger too. Over the years, different suspects, including the strip-club owner Richard's, were charged with the murders of some of the women, but no one was ever convicted. Richard's was investigated back in 1990, for robbing a sheriff's evidence room of 300 pounds of marijuana with the then chief Deputy Sheriff no less. Ethan Brown, the investigative reporter linked the prostitutes to   high-level police officers. Multiple pieces of evidence tied police to the murders, he believed, with some of the victims being both afraid of but on the verge of speaking out about police corruption. 'The Brown family accounts are corroborated by task force witness interviews; one was noted as saying that "Laconia Brown told her that three police officers were going to kill her.'

Ethan Brown believes the witnesses he spoke to, who said police were involved in murdering and disposing of evidence and bodies. At the heart of 'The Jennings 8' is the involvement of both sides of the law allegedly, with two law enforcement members who believed they were close to uncovering the truth, finding themselves accused of crimes themselves and being ousted from office. At times, evidence went missing, or the crime scenes were not investigated until well after the discovery of the bodies. News Channel 4WWL interviewed private investigator Menard in 2014, years after he began helping the families of the victims in trying to uncover proof of the murderers. "I think we have more than one killer involved; I think they all run in the same circle. I think people know something but they're afraid to talk."

There have been recent convictions of police misconduct. In 2013, Johnny Lassiter, an officer during the period of killings, pled guilty to stealing from the evidence room. Another sheriff's deputy was fired for exactly the same thing a few years earlier. The 2008 Task Force paperwork obtained by the News Channel, of over one hundred pages, held multiple witness reports of claims of officers being involved in this string of murders. Another Deputy Sheriff, Warren Gary, the chief criminal investigator on the cases, was found guilty of a 2007 ethics violation. He had sold on a truck that had reportedly been the vehicle used to transport one of the dead victims to her dumping site in the river. He had sold it on and it could not be traced. The truck would have held vital DNA and forensic evidence.

Chapter 6: Masks and Hoods

While British Newspaper The Observer pondered whether the 'Jennings's 8' case was "the real inspiration behind the first series of True Detective," there's another truly twisted case that perhaps more aptly fits the themes presented in the first True Detective Series. It is the case of Hosanna Church.

In the swamplands of Louisiana, it seemed that a true tale of clan occult rituals was unfolding, back in June 2005, when the Newspaper headlines in Louisiana read, "Deputy Sheriff to face 24 more counts in Satanic Child Sex Abuse Church Scandal."

They were referring to his alleged possession of child pornography, as well as to his participation in a cult-like group's sexual molestation of their tiny congregation's children. Deputy Sheriff Christopher Labat, 24, was being charged alongside several other members of this small Church. His charges were counts of aggravated rape of minors, and failure to report child abuse while holding a position of authority. The Church was called Hosanna Church, in Ponchatoula, not far from where filming took place for season 1 of True Detective, starring Woody Harrelson and Matthew Mcconaughey, and the deputy was one of nine adults, both male and female, who had been arrested for being suspected of having sex with children as part of their ritual worship inside the rural Church. Worship which, according to their Reverend, was of an occult nature.

Police had seized computers from the deputy Sheriff's home, and the deputy Sheriff was being held in jail. Police were searching his home, as well as those of the other suspects, for videos, photographs and any other related items.

It was alleged that the deputy Sheriff had used toys to lure children to their sexual abuse, which was believed to have begun in 1999, and continued until at least 2003, and the authorities were now in the process of going through what they said was "mountains of evidence." The police said they were planning to interview 100 people, and said that more arrests were expected to follow. Just like the story in True Detective, it would appear that depravity and the devil's work lay on both sides of the law. Along with videos and photographs, detectives said they had searched a storage unit and seized a number of trash bags filled with "costumes" and masks. Victims, as well as suspects in the case, stated that the costumes, as well as puppets, were used in the rituals which took place in the tiny rural church, with the intention of the puppets being used to encourage the children to join in the "rituals," and the Masks presumably to hid their faces. The detectives said that according to suspects' testimonies, the adults would wear black clothing and masks when they performed their blood-letting rituals, using cat's blood, which they would then rub onto the children's bodies.

It all began rather bizarrely, when the Reverend of the Church walked into the Sheriff's office and began to tell a tale that would appall and horrify the detectives. Even worse, the Reverend told it in such an unemotional way. Detective Carpenter said, "He walked into my office and sat down, just as calm as you and me talking now." He couldn't believe what happened next. "When he came in he basically thought that after he told us what he did he was just going to go on about his business of the day. In his confession, he sat down and told me, "I want to talk about the dedication to Satan of a baby."

"It floored me. You're talking about a man who professes to be a preacher and a church leader, abusing children and worshiping Satan. I thought I'd seen it all - Then something like this happens. It stays with you."

Pastor Louis Lamonica of Hosanna Church in Ponchatoula had walked into the Sheriff's office and begun to talk. For several hours, he sat with a detective. The middle aged, mild mannered Pastor started to describe what had been going on at his tiny church, hidden away in the middle of no-where. He began to relay the vilest of incidents, in which he said children were made to perform sexual activities with each other, with animals, and with the adults there. While the sexual abuse was being carried out, the Pastor and others of his small congregation would pour blood from slaughtered cats over the children's naked bodies. He said that it had been going on for several years, and that it was in service to the devil.

Although when the Church was searched, it was said that the detectives did not find the Pentagram painted on the floor that the Pastor had described, nor the blood stains; they did find traces of bodily fluids. Later, the statements would then be changed to admit they had found these things. The Public defender for the accused would also later agree that there did seem to have been some kind of sex and blood magic rituals inside the Church. Reggie McIntyre, who represented four of the defendants in the case, pointed out that there had been no physical evidence provided for trial, and that the cases were heavily reliant on testimony. He said that those accused had not carried out rape, but his defense appeared to be that "the devil cult you have here, the play with blood and all that stuff; it could be endangerment to children and could be to the point where some sexual gratification or molestation was involved."

If anyone was thinking the Pastor had decided to come clean and confess of his own volition, they would probably be wrong. A member of the congregation, which was made up of only a handful of people, had fled the County, leaving behind her husband, who she said was in on the whole thing, and had then called the police. It's most likely the Pastor had thought his confession might make things easier on himself rather than waiting for the police to come and arrest him. He would be wrong about that too, and by the time he had finished confessing, the detectives would probably have known that what he was telling them, if proven to be true, carried a death sentence in the State of Louisiana.

Witnesses when questioned later described the wearing of special robes, pentagrams drawn on the church floor, sex with a dog and the sacrifice of cats. The alleged victims were suspected to be at least twenty-five, including babies.

Along with the Pastor, a male member of the Church was found guilty of raping his own baby daughter. It was his wife who had fled the county and finally reported it, though she too faced arrest on her return. Nicole Bernard, 36, had contacted authorities and so began the investigation. Her husband, Trey Bernard, was the one who had raped his own baby   daughter.

The Sheriff, Daniel Edwards, who was himself a former state prosecutor, said that the evil group had succeeded in keeping their activities secret with "An effective formula for escaping detection: the use of a Church, and, the close-knit relationship between the members and their chosen victims, with many being related to them, ensuring that it was unlikely the victims would go to the authorities for help. They were very secretive and very good at keeping their secrets." Edwards said.

It was in the "Youth hall" behind the Church that police said that they had found a faint outline of a pentagram on the floor, still there despite efforts to scrub it away. Strangely however, when it came to the court cases for the accused, and the witness testimonies in court, there was no more mention of the "devil worshipping" activities. Rather, it was deemed to be more of an incest group. The Pastor said that he had raped his own sons. His two sons changed their testimonies in the witness box and recanted their statements that they had been raped in satanic devil worship by their own Father. Their Father, the Pastor, blamed a female member of   the congregation, who had him under her spell. He said it was all her fault. Despite the trailer full of 'evidence' including the garbage bags full of 'costumes and masks,' hundreds of computer discs, tapes and videos, the court cases had removed all trace of the occult theme behind the crimes.

The reason the trials did not focus on the satanic side of things, was because the prosecution believed it would have proven a distraction; as the assistant D.A. on the case, Don Wall said, "Devil worship" is itself not against the law. Worshipping the devil is not illegal; Child molestation is. That's what I focused on."

Parishioner Austin Bernard was convicted of raping both his own infant daughter and a twelve-year-old boy, and another child. He received 3 life sentences. Another male parishioner was also convicted of raping Bernard's infant daughter. The Pastor received four life sentences for the rape of his own two male children, as well as other children.

The Pastor described the ritual carried out with Bernard's new baby daughter; "It started like a church service but there was satanic music, dark candles burning. The baby was in this Pentagram. She was put in the middle, in a black dress." The group then reportedly began chanting around Bernard's baby daughter. The Pastor said that during such services, he would become "distorted by the devil, and demons would turn me into an animal; a spider, a wolf, a snake...."

Strangely however, despite more than 200 pages of "confessions" that he wrote before he was arrested, he never mentioned the devil or demons in it. The opinion of many of the professionals involved in the case was that he introduced the theme of satanic rituals and being taken over by the Devil, as a way of reducing and side-stepping his own culpability and as a convenient way of passing the blame.

"Trey" Bernard described to detectives how six adults would line up shoulder to shoulder and perform sex acts on his baby daughter, or other children, who were passed down the line. He said that his own wife was one of those in the line, and was one of the adults who participated in this activity, including covering the children in blood, as well as the wife of the Pastor.

"Trey" said that it was the women who coached the children in keeping their mouths shut about the abuse. As for the Pastor, he blamed his wife, and another member of the tiny congregation called Lois Mowbray, who "claimed she was a Prophet of God." He claimed she made him wear dresses and toy snakes around his neck to represent "the Pharaohs." Trey Bernard too blamed it on being controlled by this worshipper Mowabray, and by his now ex-wife too.

The Pastor confessed in recorded interviews to raping his own sons from the age of around 5 years old. He described also the "orgies" which took place at the Church and in the Youth Hall, in which his own two sons were forced to play a central role with a room full of adults. He also forced his sons to have sex with each other and animals. In his confessions he made no mention of the role of the woman who he later said made him do it all. He said she made him write down his sins and his terrible thoughts, and that's how it all began. All of the accused pleaded guilty   to their charges, apart from the Deputy Sheriff, who, although reported that child pornography was seized from his house, had his charges dropped for some reason.

Was this whole vile case a straight-forward, albeit grotesque and disgusting case of incest and abuse, with no real involvement of the devil and demons at all? It would seem very possible, and yet, for much of the time after the Pastor took over the Church, the man who owned the tire shop next door began to see that things weren't right; though he had no idea that it was anything like the reality it turned out to be. He began to grow increasingly suspicious of the activities of the coven-like handful of parishioners, who became increasingly isolationist and turned away any new members. They painted their windows solid white so that no-one could see inside. He also said that just before the Church closed for good, only weeks before the whole saga of abuse came to light, he counted 8 dump trucks arrive and cover the back lot of the Church in dirt.

What had they been wanting to hide? And, had the detectives investigating the case been aware of this? - The detectives did dig up the back yard, expecting to find buried animals; they didn't find any, but they did find what they described as "tons of potential evidence."

As to what was inside the "Youth Hall," the lead detective said there was a lot of writing on the walls, a lot of scriptures. Floor to ceiling was covered with bible writings, and yet, in terms of physical evidence, there was surprisingly little, apart from the costumes and masks. The confessions however, said it all, and as the detectives who worked on it for months said, "it doesn't really matter if the actions were done in the name of the devil or the lord; it happened."

Though the prosecution sought to minimize and play-down the Satanic occult nature of what happened in the Church, the former State Prosecutor said, "In all my thirty years, the devil-worship aspect of the case; it's the most disturbing things I've ever read."

Each member of the sick Church group, who disguised themselves with their masks and hoods, had a nickname according to those who confessed. One of them, Trish Pierson, was given the name 'Bluey-Black' said to be because of the colors on the Spell book she always carried.

In the Pastor's first confession, when he walked into the Sheriff's office, he said that there was 'Faeces laid around. There was urine;' and he claimed that during these satanic rituals he would become 'distorted' by the Devil and that demons would change him into an animal – 'a snake, a fox, wolf, spiders.'

"I could be having sex with somebody, there was urine, and because of demons, some of them literally demons ...you change...like I had wore hair...but I didn't wear fox hair."

The Detective asks him to clarify what he means, whether he means he would literally change, and he replies, "Literally. Yes. You see, you are welcoming demonic spirits." He said his face would distort. Of course, he was perhaps just lying, or exaggerating.

The culture of the Church was that they would gather together to confess their sins and talk about them out loud; after they had abused their own children in a repetitive cycle. They would hold abuse 'ceremonies' then confess to them, in twisted and screwed up mind-set.

As to whether they all got caught is a bone of contention. "There are people who made pleas in return for testifying against others who I think were more involved than we will ever know. There were kids in and out of that Church who never said they were abused, but I don't think that's at all likely. The scary thing is we only learned so much. I think it went way deeper than what the prosecutor was able to bring in. You're only seeing a very small piece of this puzzle. I think what's scary is the things we didn't find out."

What did he mean he wore hair? The things the Pastor described; the masks, the costumes, the hoods, the fur, the hair; his words are reminiscent of Courir de Mardi Gras celebrations, with the men on horses; animal masks covering their faces, and dressed in their gaudy and quite scary costumes. Courir de Mardi Gras is the traditional celebrations which takes places in Louisiana's Cajun country, dating back to the early French settlers in the swamps and prairies between New Orleans and the Texan border. Every year on Ash Wednesday, a ceremonial run is carried out with participants on foot and on horseback, and they to farms 'begging' for food and animals. Live chickens are chased to be captured for supper, all the while wearing their elaborate and gaudy costumes, their often terrifying masks, and their capuchins; the long pointed hats that rise high off their heads. There are symbolic processions and parades too, with participants dancing for their gifts of food. The celebrations are lively, colorful, and for anyone who has never seen them perhaps very scary, and yet there is nothing sinister in these parades and rituals. They do however depict the rich cultural heritage of the region, and when thinking of these costumes and the hoods and fur and 'hair' and masks of the Church group, one cannot but help remember the still photographs shown in 'True Detective', which depicted masked men from all levels of society, and the blindfold children who were being led in a secret procession by these men, to their terrible and unspeakable fate.

Chapter 7: The Wolf-Riders

In the Manchac Swamp of Louisiana; an unincorporated community in Tangipahoa Parish, in the same parish as the Hosanna Church religious cult, not only does the legend of the Rougarou; the Cajun Werewolf live on, but so too does the legend of Julia White. It's a legend of a true event, and based on the connection between the death of a Voodoo Queen and the destruction of entire villages.

White was a high priestess of Voodoo, who lived there for many decades. She lived in the early 1900's and as her powers became known, those who lived in the area would go to her house to seek her help with healing or love spells. She helped anyone who came to her, doing powerful Voodoo conjuring to summon the supernatural power to bring forth her client's requests, but it was said that her powers in the occult were so great that soon people began to regard her with suspicion and fear, wondering just what else she could do if she chose to. As she grew older, it was almost as though the local folk's superstitions toward her grew stronger, and it was only when they themselves had an urgent need th

visit her for help. In the meantime,

made sure to keep their distance from her

this seemed to isolate her even more. Althou

always kept herself to herself, as time went on she found herself constantly alone, until someone turned up with their problem and begged her to help them. Although there are no accounts of her ever using her powers to do harm to any person, it was believed that she certainly could do if she chose, and it was almost as though the locals felt she might put the evil eye on them if they got too friendly with her. They felt it safest to keep their distance.

Which came first is hard to know, but the longer she lived alone and isolated from everyone else, and the longer they avoided her, the more eccentric she appeared to become. When local people passed by her house, they began to hear her singing softly. It wasn't the sound of her voice which so disturbed them however; it was the words she used. She would sing; "On the day I die, I will take you all with me." She would sing the same line, over and over again.

...d this to the fact that she always appeared to be able to predict when something bad was going to happen to someone in the neighborhood. She would always see it coming, and she wasn't afraid of saying it. It scared the local folk, and they all hoped and prayed she wouldn't predict that harm would come to them. She was always correct in her dire predictions, and the locals wondered where this power of prediction truly came from. They believed it could be coming from evil spirits, or the very Devil himself.

In her old house on the edge of the swamp, she would sing that same song every day and people seemed to be able to hear it all around them. "On the day I die, I will take you all with me." Then she died. On the day of her funeral, just as her body was being laid to rest in the burial plot, one of her terrible predictions came true. The very words in the song she had sung every day, that put such fear into the neighborhood, turned into reality. She had vowed that for years, when her death came, she would take the entire town with her; everyone would die. Just as her body was being lowered into her grave, a violent hurricane tore through the region, tearing everything up and killing multiple people as it went. In fact, more than one town was destroyed that day. The hurricane devastated much of the residences and businesses in nearby towns too. It claimed the lives of more than one hundred people. When the worst had passed and a handful of survivors remained, Julia White's coffin had disappeared. It was no longer in her burial plot.

It was not until the water levels had gone down and the weather calm again that her body was found deep inside the Manchac swamp. Her house too had been destroyed. As for the many who had died that day, they were all buried together in a huge mass grave in the swamp. With so many bodies buried within the swamp, superstition and fear of the swamp has only increased. Those who venture into the swamp may be advised to know that, as well as more than one hundred bodies, it was also the final resting place of the Voodoo Queen, who many of those dead believed had caused the hurricane to come and kill them.

In Louisiana of course, there is also the legend of the Loup Garou, who are said to lurk within the swamps of Louisiana. The Loup Garou, or Rangou, is a creature of myth and legend who was used as the epitome of a scary monster to keep Cajun children in line; or the Loup Garou would come and snatch them away and take them into the swamp to a bloody fate. Its home is the swamp and forest and children its food, or so the old folk of Louisiana would tell their kids.

This half-animal half-man is said to have been lurking within the Louisiana swamps for centuries. The Loup Garou or Rangoooo is believed to be a shapeshifter akin to the folkloric Werewolf. The Loup Garou were said to have originated in Europe and inadvertently been brought to Louisiana by the early settlers. The creature was perhaps first recorded however in Kamouraska, on the south shore of the Saint Lawrence River in the Bas-Saint-Laurent region of Quebec, Canada.

From the annals of the Quebec Gazette, 1766, as pointed out by researcher Joseph Gagne, comes the following true report: (The language is of course antiquated.) "By accounts from St. Rock we learn that there is a Ware Wolfe wandering that Neighborhood, who, to the talent of persuading people to believe what he himself is ignorant of, and promising what he cannot perform, adds that Obtaining of what he desires. It is said that this Animal came, by the assistance of his two hind legs, to Quebec on the 17th of last month with a design to pursue His Errand. This Beast is said to be as dangerous as That which appeared last Year in the Country of Gevaudan; wherefore it is recommended to the Public have to be cautious of him as it would be of a ravenous Wolf.'

A Year later, there is another account;

On December 10th, 1767: "We learn that a Ware Wolfe who has roamed through this Province for several years, and done great destruction, with several attacks in the Month last, by different Animals. They had the Army against this monster; and in November, Animals received such furious attacks that it was thought they were entirely Delivered from this fatal Animal, who then sometime after retired into its hole. This Beast is not destroyed; it begins again to show itself, more furious than ever, and terrible havoc it makes wherever it goes - Beware of the wiles of this malicious Beast! - and take good care of falling into its Claws!"

Before these sightings, in Europe in the Middle Ages, just as with Witches and Warlocks, suspected Were-Wolves were made to stand trial too, often facing torture until they 'confessed' to their evil sins; most notably, to the accusations that they had sold their souls to the devil in exchange for the gifts of Wolf-powers. They would have all manner of torture instruments used on them and then be burnt at the stake once they had confessed.

Werewolf trials were common throughout the Middle Ages and into the Early Modern Period. Along with accusations against Witches, in Switzerland, Werewolf trials began in the Valais and Vaud regions, and it spread to many European countries including Barvaria, Austria, and Carinthia, from the 16th Century into the 18th Century. Interestingly, at the same time there were even accusations by the authorities of people being 'Wolf-riders' or 'Wolf-charmers.'

In Vaud, Switzerland, prior to the more well-known "Inquisition" a Witch-hunt on a grand scale took place. Witches and Were-Wolve accusations were interlinked, with the belief that they were inseparable supernatural activities. More than 350 people were put to death based on the allegations that they were either Witches or Were-Wolves.

According to the man known as 'Peter the chief inquisitor,' described in Thomas Wright's 'Narratives of Sorcery and Magic,' written in 1852, many witches and sorcerers 'confessed' to all kinds of terrible activities. "They made people's secrets known, and caused people to be struck by lightning or disease. Being of both sexes, they transformed themselves into wolves or other beasts in order to devour at ease. It seems that they particularly targeted children. They lay in wait, watching for opportunities to push them into rivers or any other means of causing them to have accidents, so that it would appear they had died naturally. If possible, they killed them before baptism. When buried, they dug the bodies out of the graves and carried them off to their secret rites. They boiled them in cauldrons and reduced them to liquor."

In Austria, Were-Wolf and Witch trials were held at an 800-year-old Castle. It was called Moosham Castle, also known as the Witches Castle, because of the trials that were held there. In 1715, deer and cattle were discovered slaughtered by an unidentifiable animal and Were-Wolves were suspected to be the culprits behind these killings. At first, beggars were rounded up and taken to the Castle. They were held in the dungeon and subjected to the most brutal torture using a range of barbaric instruments, with the intention of getting them to confess to their sorcery and shape-shifting into Were-Wolves. The beggars did confess, and said that they had been given a dark colored ointment from the Devil himself. This ointment had special abilities that would transform them into ferocious Were-wolves once they applied it to their bodies, they said. Once they had transformed, they would roam the countryside and attack cows or sheep, mutilating and eating them.

After their confessions, they were tortured to death or burnt. More than 130 people were accused of being shape-shifting Were-Wolves or Sorcerers, and a range of punishments inflicted including beheadings and hangings. The vast majority of these victims were male. Still a family home today, the Castle is now a major tourist attraction thought to be haunted by the souls of the tortured ones. Some of the torture implements used on the victims remain on display.

In a much more recent account, Eric Martin and his wife Shelley Rockwell-Martin perhaps have had the most well-known encounter with a 'Were-Wolf' or 'Were-Man;' Or rather, with an entire pack of them. It happened, they say, in 2007, in the small rural town of Palmyre, in Somerset County, Maine. They had just moved to the property, where Shelley would be looking after her husband following an industrial injury that had ended his career. They had found this old but picturesque farm and thought it would be just the place to take life at a slower pace. One evening shortly after moving into their new home, they were sitting on the porch, as they liked to do each evening, when they started to see lights appearing in the woods that surrounded the house. Eric thought at first that it was probably hunters with flashlights, but something made him re-consider this when the light didn't seem to display the characteristics of someone carrying a flashlight.

He decided to walk closer to the Woods to see if he could get a better look. As he approached the trees, the lights went out. The silence was unnerving and each snap of a twig under foot could be heard clearly. He entered the Wood, and yet could find no-one there nor any tracks that would have indicated hunters had been there. He felt fear like he had never known before, despite being an experienced hunter. Things just did not feel right to him.

He shook it off however when he returned to the porch, and did his best to forget about it. A couple of nights later, their dogs wouldn't go to their outside pen. They were shaking and petrified. The night was eerie enough with a heavy fog. Then they heard a strange sound in the distance, inside the Woods. It was a sound they couldn't recognize, but the danger it implied chilled them both. They went back inside the house, hearing the sound of rustling behind them as they went. They turned around as they went in and saw five sets of eyes shining out from among the trees.

Mr. Martin did not think this could be a group of bears. He was used to seeing animals at night-time on hunting trips; but this did not feel the same. Fear permeated the air. Although they were now indoors, he wanted to get his guns to protect himself and his wife, but they were out in the shed for safe-keeping. The creatures had now emerged from the Woods and were standing on their hind legs staring at the house. Their dogs were hiding in another room in the house, cowering. He attempted to go outside to bring the car closer so that he could get his wife and daughter into the car and get them to safety; he believed that from the size of the creatures, which were standing on their hind legs and at least 7-8 feet tall, they could break down the door if they chose to. When he went outside to get the car, their security motion light came on and illuminated the creatures standing within meters of him, surrounding him. He rushed back inside the house, abandoning the idea immediately. They called the police but the police didn't believe them.

They watched from the top floor of the house all night, too afraid to go to bed, and when morning came, the creatures were gone but they had stayed out there all night, scratching at the walls and doors of the house. They found huge tracks outside, which showed long claws. The tracks showed that the creatures had been walking upright; not on all fours.

Wolves? Bears? Dogmen? Or, had they created an illusory disguise to appear as creatures, when they were really of extra-terrestrial origin, or demonic inter-dimensional entities. What were the strange lights that seemed to accompany them?

Back in 1972, reports also emerged from Defiance, Ohio. The reports were of a 'Werewolf,' or 'Wolfman' on the loose. The accounts were centered around the Railroad for some reason. Rail workers had separate night-time encounters with a creature that to them could only be described as a 'Wolfman.'

One of the rail workers even claimed to have been attacked by the creature, which rather oddly was described by him as wearing jeans and carrying a long piece of timber, which he used to hit the rail worker with from behind. Two other separate night workers described seeing a creature that was upright, on its back legs and walking, covered in dark fur. Each sighting was in the early hours, and all said that the creature or 'wolf-man' vanished into the woodland surrounding the rail tracks.

A store worker in his car also came forward to say that 'it' had ran across the path of his car as he was driving in the early hours. Then it vanished at speed.

Three separate individuals went to the police and told them they had seen a large beast that appeared to look like a werewolf. The Sheriff confirmed, "We didn't release the reports to the general public or to the news media." In each of the 3 reported sightings, the description given to the police was, he said, "vague," but each of the reports closely resembled one another and had significant similarities. Each witness mentioned the hariness of the creature first, and all said it looked like a Werewolf, but the Sheriff said he was inclined to believe it was "a person wearing some disguise or a mask." He added that the witnesses said the creature had a lot of hair, "that looked natural." Although the Sheriff said he felt at first that it was a local person playing a joke on people, he did add that the height of the creature, as described by all three of the witnesses was between 7 – 9 feet tall.

The first two witnesses, Tom Jones and Ted David, who worked on the railway, both said it had huge "hairy feet," and "fangs." One of them said, it "ran from side to side," on its back legs. When Mr. Jones first saw it, he said, "I thought it was a big joke- then I saw how woolly and hairy it was - that was it for me."

After it disappeared, he said he quickly counted up the other workers on the night shift - none were missing and so he knew he could rule out any of his co-workers being behind it and playing a trick on him. At the same time that it disappeared, he said he heard a scream in the distance.

At first, it wasn't really taken seriously by the local law enforcement, according to Sheriff Don Breckler. "We're taking it seriously now however," he told reporters, as the number of sightings increased. "We are concerned for people's safety. We don't think it is a prank now," he told Ohio's The Blade.

Another man sought refuge from what he believed was the same 'thing.' In the early hours of one morning not long after the other sightings, a man went to the police station to report that something had followed him on foot along the street. While he said he didn't turn around to look at it, he could feel it getting closer, saying he had "this crawling feeling going up my back." When he arrived at the police station he was close to hysteria.

The same night, a home owner called the police for help because her friend and her were terrified. She said that for the last few nights her back door knob was being rattled and they were too terrified to go to bed. Another woman nearby also called police saying that she was going to shoot whatever was scratching at her back door, trying to get in.

Whatever it was, after some time, the reports stopped but it was never caught and the feeling was that it had to have moved on to another location....

Chapter 8: Dimensional Disappearances

In rural Rosebury, Oregon, a middle aged couple run a foster home for adult care on their own property. They are having problems however, which have made those who live there want to leave, and the couple who run it, as well as the carers who live there, are all in fear for their lives.

Surrounded by Woods, their home appears to be under attack. There is a heavy and ominous atmosphere inside the home, and for its owners, it has led to illness and great concern. For the longest time, they say that something was happening to them, inside the house and when outside too. They were drained of energy, feeling weak and ill, suffering terrible mood swings, and on the verge of breaking up. They hated venturing outside. The Woods terrified them. Inside the house they would see faces at the window. There would be terrible sounds of knocking and banging, coming from areas in the house where no-one was, or sounding like it was coming from outside the house, banging and knocking on the doors and walls. They were hearing voices that belonged to no-one living in the house.

The owner of the house, Lori, said, "Everybody's hearing voices, everybody's afraid to go to bed at night. We're having mood swings, affecting our relationships. We don't want to leave; I grew up here. Our moods change suddenly to rage. We're all getting ill. We're tired all the time. Completely drained of energy. There's banging sounds like picking up encyclopedias and dropping them."

When psychic medium Amy Allan, of Travel Channel's Dead Files arrived, the first thing that came to her was that there was a doorway. What she said about it was frightening and shocking. "It's pretty long and it goes pretty far and there's some kind of path, separate from the doorway. There are dead people on it, walking. I'm very concerned about the living people wandering into it and disappearing to other dimensions. Some living people have disappeared. There's a barrier; someone's put up protection around the property but things are still getting in. Dead people and strange creatures are getting in the home.

There's scratching on the walls. What I'm seeing coming out of the doorway are creature-like things; but I don't know what they are."

Julia, a care-giver who lives there, woke up with a bite mark on her arm. She said it looked like human teeth marks. She won't go outside near the wooded area; she says she has seen lights flashing in the Woods and does not understand why. The first time it happened, she went outside the next day expecting to see human tracks but could find no trace of a human having been there.

The psychic goes into more detail about what she can see. "There's this path that goes very far. I think that over the years, sometimes some living people have gone into this and they have disappeared. They have disappeared into other dimensions - I don't know where - I don't want to know."

"I'm seeing a creature thing; big and dark. It seems like a devil. I feel real fear. It looks like a creature scratching on the outside walls. There are all different entities. I think that some of them could be dangerous."

She drew a sketch of one of the creatures she said she could see. It looked a bit like a wolf, but it was standing upright with very, very long legs. "There was this weird person that ran out of here and then jumped out at me, and growled, and was like trying to bite my chest and my throat. They just ran away, and it was like out of nowhere."

Outside the medium takes a walk. "Someone keeps saying the word "predator" over and over again. I felt something bearing down on me, like something really large was behind me, running after me. And then I hear that predator.... I encountered several entities during my walk, but two stood out the most. First, the creature I saw trying to get into the house. It was kind of clinging to the house. It has these really long limbs that end in these claws, and fangs. And a 'haunted' dead man; when I came into the house, I saw a male laying on the floor, apparently dead. He was being tormented by something. Outside, most of the activity that's happening here is actually coming from two different places outside. The first one, it looks almost like this very long hallway. And what I saw coming out of it was these really odd, mutant animals. One, in particular, jumps on the house. He would bang on the house, scratch on the house. There was some growling. And he's been doing this for a very, very long time. What does it want? He wants in. What would happen if he came in? - Problems."

The partner of the home owner, Devlin, said, "I've come out here at night-time, and I can just feel the presence of whatever was here. Creepy, weird things, in those trees. That got me afraid. I said: "Lord Jesus Christ, leave us alone - Just leave us alone."

The psychic explains that in the Woods is a path. "It goes right through here. There were all these dead people on this path, going back and forth. Literally, back and forth on this trail. And occasionally, some of them wander off and they'll come through the house. They feed off our negativity. They want us to fight, they want to destroy your relationship. Some of them can make physical contact, and I did see a female asleep, but there was a dead person that was actually holding her, pinning her down to the bed. It was a pretty violent thing. I had one of them jump out at me, and he just ran right up in my face and he was kind of aiming towards my throat and chest area to bite me. My biggest concern though is this in-between place, and the fact that living people can, though rarely, but they can disappear into this kind of parallel dimension. These things are coming from parallel universes. Living people can disappear into this parallel dimension.

There is truly something supernatural going on that people, way long ago, before us, knew and respected and stayed away from." She tells the home owners; "I think you should move. I don't think it's safe for anyone. You're not safe outside….."

A strange story comes from England. "Something happened to me when I was about 14 years old. I live in a small rural town in England and near to my home is a Wood in which it's believed a father and a daughter's tombs are. They were said to have lived in a castle that was near to the Woods, about three centuries ago.

Me and my friends used to go in the Woods to have a smoke and get stoned and mess about. One day   we were in there getting stoned again when we stood on some mud. This was a bit weird because we were having a hot summer. We kicked the mud around at each other and then spotted the bones. Without thinking, I picked them up; they were big and I thought they had to be bones from a bull or a cow. We decided to take them home and take them to school to show the teacher when we had science next. I put them into my rucksack and when I got home I put them out in the shed in the back garden and forgot all about them.

A few days later, strange things started to happen in the house. When we were in the lounge in the evenings, we started to hear soft voices, whispering. One time, we'd been out all day and when my brother's friend came round the next day she asked why we hadn't let her in. My brother told her we'd been out all day and she said, "No; I could see someone standing in the bedroom looking out the window."

We went in my brother's bedroom, but nothing was out of place. We couldn't understand that. About a week later, we went back in the Woods to smoke again, and my friend remembered about the bones we'd taken. I told him about what had been happening in the house and they thought I was just stoned and was joking. I told them I wasn't joking. We found the exact spot where we'd found the bones and immediately we could see there was a huge hole in the mud. There were more big bones in there.

This wasn't making sense; even though I presumed they'd been cow bones, there weren't any cows around here, and there were no other animals that big in the Woods in England. We started trying to figure out where the bones had come from and what they were and as we turned to leave, feeling a bit freaked out, my friend spotted a carved symbol like a strange star, carved into the nearest tree.

As soon as I got home I took the bones out of the shed and burnt them in the back garden. The strange things in the house started to get worse. We would hear footsteps like someone coming up the stairs when we were all in bed at night. My sister began to see fleeting dark shadows that were huge. Radios in the house would come on at full blast in the middle of the night.

I'm in my late 30's now, and it's still happening, even though I moved out of that house years ago. It happens in my house now. Apparently, after doing some research at the Library all those years ago, I discovered that the Woods had a dark history of being used for black magic and Witchcraft. The thing was, I don't think that symbol had been on the tree when we found the bones and so it still had to have been happening when we used to smoke in the Woods. Apparently, after researching online, the exact design of that symbol meant something; it meant that you had pissed someone off and it was like a warning.

My last relationship ended quite quickly, just like my other ones. My girlfriend got too scared to sleep at my house. She got too scared to even be around me.....'

Chapter 9: Gothic Macabre Disappearance

Home of Edgar Allan Poe, Massachusetts, New England, is an area steeped in creepiness, paranormal happenings, legends and lore. 'The Marsh People' are said to live in the Cape Cod region and these entities are said not to be shadow people; but people who appear solid in mass and are the color of the mud from which they emerge; solid forms who climb from the mud beneath them.

The 'Marsh People,' or 'Swamp People' go back to the 1800's, when it was said they would climb out of the marshes and drag a passing horse or traveler down into the mud to their doom. Could they merely be the cause of illusions and mirages? Hunters within the swamp have the opinion that they are more than illusions. Some reports claim that people have disappeared while inside the swamp. While this could be explained by the sinkholes and sinking mud, maybe that is not always the case.

These 'Marsh People' are said to have taken to the swamps when the Settlers arrived, and it is now their descendants who crawl through the mud and emerge to claim a hunter or hiker, who has no idea they have wandered into terrain that the Swamp People consider to be theirs. The Swamp People emerge from the mud, hunting for human flesh and claim those who trespass there.

Perhaps one of the strangest true mysteries that occurred within the New England area however, is that of the odd disappearance and death of Edgar Allan Poe. The famous literary figure whose writing was of the finest gothic macabre, was himself the central figure of his own mysterious disappearance and subsequent demise.

On September 27th, 1849, Mr. Poe disappeared. He reappeared six days later, where he was found in the street, delirious, in great distress and completely incoherent. Gone was his dapper and refined clothing, and in its place were filthy clothes and scruffy, dirty shoes. Neither his clothes nor his shoes fitted him. He was rushed to a medical facility where he was kept in isolation, and where he lapsed into a fevered state and was barely conscious until his hasty death arrived. No-one was ever able to determine what had happened to him, or where he had been in the days he had been missing.

Many scholars, academics and historians have attempted to find the definitive answer to his unexplained disappearance and his very odd return, and while there are a number of theories of merit, the cause remains still unproven.

There is mystery within this mystery, such as the missing medical notes, the conflicting accounts given by friends and acquaintances, and the words Poe managed to say before he died. Perhaps he was the victim of simple foul play, although he did not appear to have any obvious wounds when he reappeared, and where had he been kept for the days in which he had been missing? If he had been kept somewhere, why would that have been?

When he was discovered in an Inn on the main street in Baltimore, an acquaintance by the name of Joseph Walker sent an urgent letter to one of Poe's friends, requesting his help. The letter he wrote to the friend, Dr Joseph Snodgrass, an editor, said, "The gentleman is rather worse for wear and appears in great distress.

He says he is acquainted with you, and he is in need of immediate assistance from you." He later described Poe as wearing an expression of "vacant stupidity which made me shudder. He had evidently been robbed of his clothes. So stupefied, we had to carry him out as if a corpse."

Later, he would go on to explain that Poe was indeed terribly intoxicated; however, when his original letter is scrutinized it does not appear that this was the case, and later he would be accused of exaggerating or twisting the truth to make it appear that the great writer had indeed merely been totally drunk.

To anyone that had known the smartly and stylishly dressed Poe, the description he gave of the literary figure must have come as a complete shock. He described Poe as having "vacant eyes," and was "unwashed, haggard, unkempt and repulsive."

When Poe was taken to the nearest infirmary, the head doctor there, Dr John Moran, for some reason confined the famous writer to his own room in a part of the hospital usually used for drunks. In this room the writer is then observed to veer from unconsciousness to delirium in which he talks aloud constantly as though to imaginary people, and appears to see imaginary objects. He is still unable to explain what has happened to him or where he has been.

When Poe was in his dingy room, he reportedly repeatedly called out someone's name. He called out for a person called "Reynold's" and yet no-one could find out who this person was. The Dr. tried to find out from Poe's friends and family who this person could be, but no-one knew of any person by that name. When the Dr. tried to reassure Poe by telling him that soon his friend would soon visit him, the writer's response apparently was to tell the Dr: "The best thing he could do would be to blow out his brains with a pistol."

He died in the room on October 7th, his final words according to the doctor being; "Lord help my poor soul." Disturbingly, no records of Poe's death exist. All have somehow been lost, if they ever did exist. His cause of death ranged from the theories of alcohol; though there appears to be no corroboration that this could have been the case. There were rumors that the writer was particularly unable to hold his drink and so the slightest imbibing of alcohol would lead to heavy intoxication; others disputed this and said he rarely drank. He also belonged to a Temperance movement, which again would appear to contradict the theory that he drank himself to death. Some wondered if he was a user of Opium, but most who knew him also felt this was wholly unfounded. Others suggested he died of congestion on the brain or a brain tumor. Perhaps he had Cholera, Meningitis or Rabies, although one would have thought perhaps the hospital he died in would have noted his symptoms if he did. The most likely scenario perhaps is that given he was found on the day of an Election, he had been the victim of 'Cooping.' This was a sinister practice of abducting victims off the street, and through force and threats of violence, making them vote in multiple towns in the area, while drugged.

People would be targeted, snatched off the street by a gang and taken away where they would be drugged and forced to vote for the person behind the vote-rigging method. While this has perhaps become the most realistic cause of his sudden disappearance and re-mergence, and one that has been mentioned in many biographies, those who disagree with the theory cite the fact that he was a widely recognized figure, even if he had been dressed in an outfit he would never have been seen wearing. His face was still instantly recognizable and it didn't seem possible that he could have been led to voting stations and not been recognized by officials or voters there as he went in to vote. Also, he appeared to have no signs of injuries that might have been expected from a struggle with abductors.

Others have suggested he was victim of a robbery which had left him insensible for days, but he was still grasping an expensively crafted walking cane when found. What perhaps is most strange is that he was not allowed any visitors when confined in the hospital. Though a cousin arrived to see him, he was turned away. Details are scant and this itself is mysterious, because despite the voluminous publications about Poe's life, the in-depth accounts of the end of his life are sorely lacking and the mystery of his inexplicable disappearance remain.

Chapter 10: The Canyon Mystery

Seeking notoriety and reward, a newlywed couple set out on the most daring of adventures. Their plan after it succeeded, was said to have been to set out on a lecture tour, commanding well-earned fees for their public speaking, as they regaled their audiences with their tales of daring-do. They would become lauded celebrities, recognised among the most adventurous explorers ever known.

Photographs taken just before they set off showed their fierce and fiery determination and they looked like Bonnie and Clyde, well on their way to conquering the world in a legal but very daring way. Unfortunately, it didn't work out that way.

Only just newly-wed, this young couple chose to eschew a traditional romantic honeymoon and replace it with the high-risk adventure of rafting down the rapids of the Colorado River, intent on enabling wife Betty to claim the world record as the first woman to ever make the treacherous trip. They were also going to attempt to beat the fastest record.

It was November 1928 when they set out, having fully planned their trip and adequately prepared for their requirements. They had a small scow; a flat-bottomed boat used for the purpose of transporting cargo and rafting. It was approximately 20 feet in length, weighed 2 tons, and was of the type commonly used at the time for river rafting. Her husband Glen had built it himself. They loaded it with the provisions they believed they would need for their trip, which began at Hermit Rapids, and set off. A month later, their scow was found without them in it. It was floating upright and still had their provisions in it. It had no damage to it; but the newly-wed couple had disappeared. Somehow, they had simply vanished. They hadn't disappeared immediately; at River Mile 231 into the journey, the scow was discovered empty. Inside the raft, was Bessie's journal, which she had kept as they had progressed on their journey.

They had last been seen on November 18th at the 165 River Mile mark. That was the last notation in her journal. Somehow, after that, they had both vanished into thin air. Prior to this, they had made sure to keep their respective families informed of their progress, and had ensured that the Newspapers and Photographers were charting their progress. They would be spending almost 7 weeks in their attempt and they wanted media coverage all the way.

On the day they disappeared, they were ahead of schedule. They had been making excellent progress on their journey. It was Thanksgiving and so they stopped off to celebrate with a dinner. When it was later discovered that they had gone missing at some point after that evening, a massive search was started which made national headlines, but it never turned up a single trace of the couple. As soon as Glen's father heard that they had disappeared from their raft, he commissioned a huge search party. Despite it being winter, and in some of the roughest terrain, a massive effort was made to find them. Determined to find his son and new daughter-in-law, he hired specialist searchers to go into the Canyon to look for any signs that they were on land, but trackers could find no indications they had left the water. Every part of the Canyon was thoroughly searched in the area where they had been known to last be, and the   area where their scow was later found. There was nothing that could provide any explanation. The search lasted for weeks, and into months, and the river was searched for their bodies. They could have fallen in, or been dragged in somehow, and yet the water did not give up their bodies; bodies surface after around ten days, if they are not weighted down by something, and nothing was missing from their scow – nothing had fallen in and dragged them in with it. Nothing appeared to be at all disturbed on their raft. It was all exactly in order. The speculation rose that perhaps one of them had fallen in and the other had dived in to try to save them, but then where were their bodies? Searches continued for months.

Between the point where the raft and her Journal were found, and the last place they were spotted on their raft, was a notorious rapid. In fact, it was known to be the most dangerous part of the river. Mile 232 was known to be called 'The Fangs' because of a set of very sharp rocks that lay in low level water and had in the past snagged many rafts. Neither of them had life preservers; though they were available, the pair had opted not to take them on their trip, perhaps adding to the thrill of their adventure. It was agreed that they could easily have got into trouble at this point if the boat had hit the upright Fangs, and yet their boat, when it was found, showed no signs whatsoever of any collision or damage. It didn't seem that it could have been these rocks then that had caused their disappearance; if the boat was not damaged, and their bodies not found in the water, it appeared they must have successfully cleared that part of the river.

The stress of attempting their adventure, fraught with such danger, led to the presentation of one theory behind their disappearance as being that one had killed the other after a ferocious row, and then fled to avoid capture by the authorities. The problem with this theory however was that it was Winter, in the middle of hostile terrain, and the chance of surviving on the run was slim to none. Besides which, where was the dead body if that had been the case?

Strangely, many years later while on a group rafting trip, an elderly lady confided in the others on the trip that she was in fact the missing Bessie, and she spun a tale of having stabbed her brute of a husband dead, faked her own death, and made her escape to live a life under the guise of another name. The problem with her confession however was that when her background was looked into, and it was easily verified, she couldn't possibly have been Bessie.

After the death of well-known and highly successful female rafter Georgie Clark in the 1990's, speculation grew that she could have been Bessie. Georgie was actually born Bessie DeRoss, but was discovered to have changed her name to Georgie. Again however, her background was easily verified and again she turned out not to be the other Bessie. When a skeleton was found in the 1970's with a bullet hole in its skull, it was believed that this could have been the missing husband. At first the authorities were suspicious of a photographer, because the skeleton had been found on his property in the Canyon. He was also known to have been one of the last people to have actually seen the couple. However, forensic testing soon ruled out Glen as being the skeleton because the results showed that the person   whose skeleton it was, had died decades after the couple had gone missing.

A camera recovered from the raft revealed that the final photo the couple had taken was on or about November 27. When they disappeared, they were just 40 miles away from the end of their trip, so close to having completed it. Still today, no-one knows what happened to them. Glen's father was of the opinion that they had probably run into some kind of difficulty with their raft and had disembarked and attempted to hike their way out of the Canyon. He believed they had got lost and then died in the woods somewhere. If that were the case: where were their skeletons?

Chapter 11: "How can a woman just vanish?"

"Is it just a coincidence that her baffling vanishing took place a stone's throw from a place closely associated with programs designed to make people disappear?"

"The truth is; none of it makes any sense," Kerry Bauchiero told reporters; "And that's the hardest part." She was talking after the discovery of her Mother's body. She wasn't the only one to make such comments. "This one has really got us all stumped," Steve Mitman, a volunteer with Franklin County Search and Rescue said, one week into the search for the missing woman. "Like a spacecraft popped down and picked her up," he said.

The missing woman had become lost somewhere in western Maine, in the thick forest between Saddleback Mountain and Sugarloaf Mountain. She was believed to be North of Saddleback in the Range, south of Rangeley. She was exceptionally prepared; she had taken a course at the Appalachian Trail Institute, and to ready herself for her expedition she had also undertaken a 200-mile practice hike. In advance of this trip, she had even made Excel spreadsheets, to plan every step of her hike down to the infinitesimal detail.

An experienced hiker, she was in the Appalachians with her hiking partner, another female, walking the 2,200 Appalachian Trail as part of a 'bucket list.' She was following in the footsteps of travel writer Bill Bryson who later wrote of his journey in 'A walk in the Woods.' They had planned to cover 1,165 miles on their hike, back in April 2013, until her partner was called home due to a family crisis and she vowed to continue on alone. By this stage, they had already been hiking for nine weeks, without any incident. Although she was now 66 years old, her hiking partner described her as "a scrupulous planner, who always knew where to find water." In fact, when her body was found, much later, one of her bottles still had water in it. When she disappeared, she had already covered nearly 1,000 miles of the trail.

Geraldine Largay's plan when she went missing, had been to hike eight miles to the Spaulding Mountain lean-to, and spend the night there, then continue up the trail another 13.5 miles to where it intersects with Route 27. Her husband George was going to be waiting for her there. When she didn't arrive by late afternoon, he presumed she was delayed by perhaps rain, so he spent the night in his car. By Wednesday afternoon, his wife still hadn't arrived, so he stopped a police car that was passing by and the search began.

The searchers first checked the trail and the thick forest 100 feet on either side of the trail. Then they expanded the search to include the side trails, the small roadways, and the streambeds between her last known location and the destination she was known to be heading to. In all, dozens of trained S&R as well as volunteers covered 30 miles, as the days passed without any sighting of her. The next 7 days, dogs as well as horses were brought in, Helicopters flew overhead; but they could find no trace of her, or any indication where she might be.

Her son in law, Ryan, said, "If something had happened to her on the trail, she would have known to stay put, and someone would have found her; clearly something other than that happened."

A mystery woman was claimed to have phoned a ranger's station telling them to tell the missing woman's husband that his wife would not be meeting him at their pre-arranged rendezvous. Despite much being made of this mysterious caller and her message, since then however, a spokesman for the Park Rangers and Police stated that there was a mix-up in this message, and that it did not in fact relate to the missing woman at all. What no-one could understand however, was how this woman had seemingly completely vanished. Her husband stayed there for two weeks, desperately joining the search effort to try to find her. Maine Warden service and other official agencies had instigated an immediate full-blown search for her. In fact, it turned into the biggest search in the history of Maine. Scores of hikers were interviewed to find out if any of them had information that could help them locate her. No-one was able to help. Two years later, her body was found; 3 miles from where she had last been known to be, and a 10-minute walk from a dirt trail that   led to a road. The rescuers had never found her, despite covering that ground looking for her. They had searched the precise area in which she had been discovered.

"The area she was discovered in was described as being so densely forested that only trained Park Wardens had been allowed to search there," US Newspapers said. That sounded perfectly reasonable; after all, no-one would have wanted serious injuries or even fatalities to happen to volunteers or rescuers as a result of conducting a search for someone in a wilderness area. The thing was, when she was found the searchers had been remarkably close to the spot she was in; in fact, it seemed impossible for them not to have come across her as they searched. Also, if the spot was so inaccessible to all but the most highly trained Park wardens, then how did she manage to get into the area herself? And, if it really was that inaccessible, why would she have attempted to get into it anyway? When her body was discovered, there was evidence that she had been building a fire and she had made a flag from a branch of one the trees that surrounded her. She was desperately trying to draw the attention of her rescuers. Sadly, despite this, her rescuers never found her.

In December 2014, the Boston Globe had asked, "How can a woman just vanish?" When she was finally found, the Daily Mail report was as following; "Wardens say the fact that her remains were inside a sealed tent likely meant that the search dogs were unable to pick up her scent." This, one would imagine, could quite easily be challenged by a dog handler. A tent is hardly a concrete barrier; and in fact, dogs can pick up scents in urban environments where there is a multitude of thick barriers such as concrete. A tent then, would seem a rather flimsy barrier with which to create an impenetrable block that erased all chance of her scent carrying through it.

Though being only ten minutes from the main trail, for Geraldine herself, she had tragically resigned herself to never being found, after an excruciating twenty-six days of being alone and alive but somehow lost in the Appalachians. This we now know from the heartbreaking diary and last message she left for her family.

"When you find my body, please call my husband and my daughter." She had tried to call her husband when she realized that she had got lost. Her cell phone had no signal. She had moved to higher ground in an effort to reach a signal but still to no avail. Her text messages sat in her outbox, unsent.

The last notes in her diary were written on the 18th of August. Incredibly, she had been alive since July 24th; alone and lost, but still alive. She was to remain lost but no longer alive until two years had passed, when her body was found just 3,000 feet from the trail she had been hiking on, by a contractor who had been carrying out a forestry survey. Where she was found was Navy land, and in a cruelly ironic way, the land is actually part of a U.S. Navy survival skills training facility. Its use; for Survival, Evasion, Resistance, and Escape. It's a program run by the Navy.

The cause of the missing lady's death was determined to have been as a result of starvation and exposure to the elements. After her body was found, social media took to discussing the tragedy. The comments were enlightening to say the least. Those who knew the hiking territory there very well, having hiked it themselves, some multiple times, commented that although the official searches for her were deemed to have been so difficult because of the heavily forested and precarious terrain that it was "impossible for anyone not trained to access it," the question that most arose was; how, given that she was so close to the trail, was she not found? Much was made of how well-marked the trail was too; in other words, people couldn't understand how, if she had got lost, she had not been able to find her way back to the trail, despite remaining alive for 28 days.

"It's marked like a Super-highway," were the comments of several local people. Then there were the comments remarking that when hiking it, "You're never very far from other people," and, "Day after day you'll encounter the same hikers."

Of course, it wasn't that Geraldine got lost on the trail; she had stepped off the trail because it was believed she needed to relieve herself and of course, did not wish to do that where there was the chance a group of hikers would come wandering by. Some have said that she made a fatal error in stepping off the path; however, others have found the entire story completely inexplicable and highly strange.

It's not that they can't understand how she became lost; it is densely covered by trees, and she had stepped off the trail, and a couple of turns and it's understandable to become disoriented in seconds and set off in the wrong direction, without realizing it. However, the detractors from the commonly spun explanation for her demise, do point out that the trails are incredibly well-marked, and very obvious. And there are many. She was not a fool; she was an experienced hiker, and her age is irrelevant; she had managed to cover more than 1,000 miles already and she was a sensible and level-headed lady. She had full prepp'd for her trip, even had an Excel spreadsheet, and, she categorically demonstrated her preparedness by surviving for more than three weeks, with water still in a bottle when her body was found.

The question is, how did she manage to survive for three weeks, just 3,000 feet; that is, just half a mile, from the nearest trail, and so close from where the extensive, comprehensive, exhaustive and very long-lasting search effort was said to have been initiated? It was the largest search in the history of the State of Maine. How could she not have been found?

The search was said to have extended to almost a 30-mile radius. A search grid that triangulated from her last known location, which was believed to have been 2 miles from where she was found, would surely have included that exact spot where she had set up her tent and given up on ever being found?

It would transpire that the search dogs had come within 100 feet of her. Why would it be that the dogs could not detect her scent? Was she really there all that time?

Where she settled was not Parks property however, despite it not being fenced off. Had the searchers perhaps avoided that Navy-owned land? Had they not searched there because it did not belong to them? And yet surely, they would have asked permission to extend their search onto the Navy land, given that it was within the National Park itself?

When the search began for Geraldine, it was said to have been severely hampered because only the fittest and most highly trained park rangers could enter the terrain she was believed to be in and volunteers were said to have not been up to the task. And yet, described in the Daily Mail as "The harrowing moment the remains of missing hiker were discovered," a film crew for the TV show Animal Planet were the ones who happened to stumble upon her collapsed tent and her body inside, and who also, perhaps rather distastefully, caught the moment on tape when a shaken Warden accompanying them opens up the tent to find her remains. How had the TV production crew managed to stumble across her tent and body inside when it was supposed to have been the most difficult area to access?

The Warden service said in their statement; "The search was one of the most unique and challenging search and rescue efforts ever to have taken place in Maine." Apparently, this was because the terrain in which she was found, which had been specifically chosen by the Navy for its remoteness and difficulty in accessing. That was why they ran their survival skills training programs there; to train their personnel in 'Evasion and Escape.' And yet, if it was so difficult to access; how had Geraldine managed to get into the area in the first place, as well as a TV crew?

"Not mentioning SERE (Survival, Evasion, Resistance and Escape) facility's existence goes beyond irresponsibility into potential complicity; someone has to explore it." This came from reporter Chris Busby, of the Bangon Daily News, who had helped Hutch Brown in researching an article he published in Maine's The Bollard independent news journal, with its introduction asking, "What role did a covert Navy "Torture school" play in the disappearance of Largay?

Busby says, "She vanished right where the trail borders this secretive Navy training facility infamous for its program's association with torture."

It seems that Brown & Busby did the research no-one else seemed to do; because, they said, there was no mention from the Wardens or law enforcement of the fact that she had strayed into Navy property, and into an area that had once been inextricably associated with "torture." Perhaps their reporting is rather overblown in hyperbole and drama in all reality, however, Busby says; "Here's some of the facts about this case: Other than fellow hikers, most accounted for; the only other people in the area when she vanished were at this facility. Some of the trainees there are not enlisted; rather, they're private contractors; and 'soldiers of fortune;' capable of bad behavior."

He continues, "In the late 1970's, a Navy diver escaped the facility and told of having been tortured there. People did not want to believe that the Government was torturing its own soldiers."

The reason why the missing lady could easily have got onto Navy land, according to them, is because, 'The boundaries are not shown on most maps, including many of the commonly used guides. Though the nearby Railroad trail has signs warning against trespass, approaching from a different route, the borders are not fenced, and there are no signs alerting hikers.'

'Within a few hundred yards of the trail she was on soldiers of fortune run around the Woods in a war-game, captured, handed over to interrogators, subjected to beatings and sleep deprivation. Just coincidence her baffling vanishing took place a stone's throw from programs designed to make people disappear?'

He is laying this possibility on a bit thick surely? I mean, could something like that really happen? Hutch Brown, the investigative reporter says he spoke to a local guide. He doesn't believe her body was there all the time it was missing. "If it were, the birds would've told me - If you die in the woods, you become a lot of things' dinners. They would have been there, feeding."

Liaison to the public at the facility, Sheldon Prosser, told the reporter there was no training happening when she disappeared, and added that participants are never alone there; although they may believe they are - they're being closely tracked, he said. He also added that there was a "significant ridge line" separating trainees from the trail area. In other words, they couldn't easily travel into the National Park land without realizing it. Likewise, that would surely then apply to anyone entering the facility via the ridge line? He told the reporter he wasn't sure if they had been informed of her disappearance, or the land searched.

Lt. Adam, spokesperson for the Warden Service, told the reporter; helicopter pilots searching for her spotted small fires inside the facility, and later determined that the facility's trainees had set them. In other words, there is conflicting opinion about whether there was training taking place, or not, according to who was spoken to. Clarity around this matter it seems probably won't be forthcoming, and though it's a good theory about her disappearance, perhaps it veers toward the conspiracy angle a little too much; but then, who really knows?

The mystery phone call that police later said was not mysterious at all, was made to the motel in which her husband had spent the night. His wife had meant   to stay there with him, but she had never made it. The female caller implied that she had spent the night with his wife at the lean-to where it was known the missing woman had planned to stay the night before she rendezvoused with her husband. The message was that his wife would be late arriving there at the motel the next night. The Park Wardens and the police were of the opinion that somehow the message got miscommunicated; either the female caller made a mistake, or the Motel manager who took the message. On the other hand, how did the message in fact turn out to be correct? in that his wife was late; very late. She never made it there. How would someone know he was there, and that his wife was planning to meet him there, unless they had been with his wife? Was it an innocent enough message from a fellow hiker his wife had met at the Lean-to shelter? Or, was there some kind of foul play involved in it after all? But then if so, how did it relate to his wife becoming lost and spending 28 days surviving out in the Woods?

The mystery is indeed perplexing and baffling. How does someone survive in the woods for 28 days, and yet never manage in all that time to find their way back to the heavily-populated trail? How did the largest search in Maine fail to find her when she was only 3,000 feet off the trail, despite their 30-mile radius search? How did a TV crew manage to stumble across her body and yet the Park Warden's say it was too difficult for all but the most highly trained searchers to get into the area she was found in?

Something just doesn't seem to add up here......

In June 2016, the body of a man who had been missing for months was found on Glen Coe mountain, an area of outstanding natural beauty on Rannoch Moor in the Scottish Highlands. The missing man, Robin Garton, in his '60's, had travelled up from South-West England to meet with friends. An experienced hillwalker, he was last seen when he checked out of his hotel in the morning. He failed to meet up with his friends two days later, as he'd arranged. When it was realized that he may be missing, the police found his car parked up in a car park close to Coire Nam Beith and they believed it most likely he had been planning to walk in the scenic area. Search and Rescue were out looking for him as soon as his car was found, with the Mountain Rescue involved as well as the police. They employed a dog unit as well as air support from the Coastguard helicopter rescue team of Inverness.

A month later, searches were still being carried out for him. Divers too were involved, but despite such major searches, no sign of him could be found. He had vanished on September 25.th On November 11th his walking poles, or at least, the police said they believed they could have been his, were found. Expensive telescopic poles had been recovered in the area where searches had been extensively carried out for weeks. A hiker had independently come across them while out walking and had taken a photograph of them. They then sent the photographs to the Mountain Rescue Team. Despite Search and Rescue returning to the area to search it one more time, they still found no sign of the missing man or any other clues.

Fast forward to June 2016, and members of Glencoe Mountain Rescue Team recovered his body from Coire nam Beith, where they had been searching for months, after emergency services were alerted by a member of the public. The same Newspaper reported on the body of another missing walker found in May in the Cairngorms National Park in the Highlands. Jim Robertson had gone missing in March. Three other walkers were still missing however. Visitor German Goffredo Bondanelli had been missing for more than a month after going on a camping trip in the area. Eric Cyl and Tom Brown had also not returned from trips in the Steall area of Lochaber last year and have still not been found. They had set out on separate hikes and were not travelling together.

Lochaber Mountain Rescue Team said: "We have now covered all potential routes that either of these missing persons could have taken from their last known locations. A rucksack belonging to Mr. Brown was found less than a mile east of Steall Falls in the Glen Nevis area on 9 July.

Ominously, the Aberdeen Press Journal wrote: 'Rescuers urge caution and vigilance as numbers still missing or found dead increases.....'

I hope you enjoyed this collection. If you have had a creepy, strange, or inexplicable experience, please do feel free to contact me.

I am actively continuing to research & collect the strangest of stories, and would be very interested to hear yours.

Thank you

Steph Young Author (facebook)

Stephenyoungauthor@hotmail.com

Also by Stephen Young:

Encounters with the Unknown

Dead in the Water; Forever Awake

The Case of the Smiley Face Killers

Something in the Woods is Taking People

Hunted in the Woods

Nightmares in the Woods

52187976R00107

Made in the USA
San Bernardino, CA
13 August 2017